EAT
ITALY

The complete companion to Italy's cuisine and food culture

CONTENTS

INTRODUCTION

Everyone loves Italian food. But how did the Italians come to eat so well? Popular culture tells us that the answer lies in the vineyards and olive groves of Tuscany – among sun-weathered peasants and grandmas serving pasta under the pergola. Yet this nostalgic fantasy has little to do with the real history of Italian cuisine.

Italian food originates in one of the richest urban cultures on the planet. By the 12th century, the Italian peninsula was the most urbanised region in the world, with huge self-governing city-states and an exploding population. The ensuing Renaissance unleashed some staggering culinary creativity, as cooks serving in powerful aristocratic households networked tirelessly to source exciting ingredients and come up with impressive dishes. It's no coincidence that so many Italian products and dishes are named after cities: *risotto alla Milanese, bistecca alla Fiorentina, prosciutto di Parma, saltimbocca alla Romana* and *pizza Napoletana*.

The Italian pantry has also been shaped by the peninsula's challenging topography. Italy was never a naturally rich or fertile place. Some 40% of the country is mountainous, and internal travel was historically hard given the saw-toothed Apennines that run the length of the country and split it in two. In the south, there are volatile volcanoes – Vesuvius, Etna and Stromboli – while the central region, which sits on the intersection of the Eurasian and African tectonic plates, is prone to earthquakes. In fact, only 28% of Italy's land is arable and most of that is located in the Po Plain, the fertile river valley that stretches from Turin to Venice across the north of Italy and down to Bologna and Rimini.

These realities have dictated Italy's uniquely diverse regional cooking, where striking differences can be found from valley to valley, village to village. This is the result of centuries of human labour and ingenuity aimed at devising unique ways to coax tasty food out of the local terroir. Take Liguria's Unesco-protected *muretti* (dry-stone walls), a 2000km (1243-mile) system of terraces created along steep sea cliffs in order to farm vines, basil and olives – an amazing feat of engineering in an unforgiving landscape.

Given the challenges here to internal trade and transport, as well as the country's 7500km (4660-mile) coastline ringed by once-powerful trading cities like Genoa, Pisa, Amalfi, Palermo and Venice, it's hardly surprising that Italian food is a sophisticated fusion cuisine. Just think of the Middle Eastern character of Sicilian couscous and *caponata*, Venice's devotion to Scandinavian salt cod, the 'Jewish-style' artichokes beloved of Romans, the Swiss-style *fonduta* of the Valle d'Aosta and the abundance of 'New World' ingredients like tomatoes and peppers in Neapolitan dishes.

Italian food tastes so *modern* because it demonstrates a forward-thinking sensibility. The Italian cook has always had a deep respect for the limits and opportunities of the local environment, combined with a talent for specialisation and a curious and creative mindset. This story continues to evolve in Italy's great cities, where a new generation of cooks, farmers, immigrants and entrepreneurs are experimenting with the latest trends and ingredients, and passionately advocating that good food made with respect is the route to health and happiness.

HISTORY & CULTURE

According to an international YouGov study conducted in 2019, Italian cuisine is the most popular in the world – and some people firmly believe that our health, environment and quality of life may depend on the lessons that Italy's food history has to offer.

How can we talk about Italian food when discussing dishes as diverse as Sicilian *caponata* (sweet-and-sour aubergine with pine nuts, raisins and vinegar), the meat-filled tortellini from Bologna or Milan's saffron-scented risotto? We can't. And, yet, Italian food is not simply some motley collection of regional dishes that were re-branded as a national cuisine when the country was unified in 1871.

Foods such as pasta, polenta and parmesan are, indeed, shared across regions – but, more importantly, it is the culture around food that truly defines Italian cuisine. Italians eat so well because eating enriches their sense of where they come from and who they are. Food isn't simply fuel here: it is a sacred communion with family and friends, and an intangible connection to place and identity.

ORIGIN STORY

Italians sometimes refer to their 'civilisation of the table'. This civilisation has deep roots, stretching back to pre-Roman times when the Etruscans reclined on couches eating multi-course meals and when, in Sicily, the Greek-speaking Mithaecus penned the first cookbook in the Western world. The Etruscans were sophisticated agriculturalists. They ate little meat and cultivated chickpeas, barley, millet and spelt, with which they made an early version of polenta. Their banquets featured fish, game birds, sheep's cheese, olives, nuts and honey. Guests dressed in fine clothes, slaves served wine in silver bowls and musicians enlivened proceedings by playing tortoiseshell lyres. This was a people practised in the art of living well.

Many of these refined Etruscan dining habits were assimilated by the Romans during their rise to power in the 4th century BCE, and by the latter days of the Republic, maintaining the food supply to Rome had become a major political issue. Because of the importance of land, the Romans also idealised produce: cereals, leafy greens, vegetables and fruit. Thanks to the Greek cultivation of olive trees in the south there was a wide variety of olives, while truffles and mushrooms were foraged frequently. Nut and fruit trees from the Levant were widely propagated: cherry trees came from Pontus (Turkey), peaches from Persia (Iran), apricots from Armenia and damsons from Syria.

As the Empire expanded, new trade routes brought spices from India and the Arabian Peninsula, while extensive pan-European military operations imported culinary knowledge from other regions. For example, the bread of the beer-drinking Gauls was admired for its quality, a result of the brewers' yeast employed in its baking. In Rome, there were farmers' markets, inns and bars, and religious festivals honouring important foods and food-making equipment, such as Fornacalia (Festival of Ovens) and the Festival of Vesta, dedicated to the goddess of the hearth.

Roman Christianity sacralised bread, wine and oil. And although meat and fish were a part of the Roman diet at all levels of society, excessive meat consumption became a mark of impious decadence and paganism, given the high meat consumption of 'barbaric' Germanic tribes. Even today, you'll notice that vegetables are viewed with reverence by Italian cooks, and are never thought of as just an accompaniment to the main meat or fish.

Left: A Roman victory banquet

THE GREAT UNIFIER: PASTA

Pasta is one of the great unifying motifs in Italy's gastronomic mosaic. But it takes on very different forms in different parts of the country. The basic meaning of the word simply means 'paste', indicating a pastry or dough made from flour and water. Pasta can be made in any number of ways – rolled, cut, extruded and filled – and there are at least 300 different shapes, each evolved to complement particular local ingredients, sauces and cheeses.

Pasta comes in two forms: fresh and dried. The former, often made with eggs, is cooked as soon as it's made and includes lasagne (sheets), tagliatelle (flat strips) and tortellini (stuffed parcels). These pastas are typical of the central and northern parts of the country and were certainly known by the Romans. Southern Italy, however, favours the chewier, high-gluten dried pasta, which is made from durum wheat and was introduced to Sicily by the Arabs, who ruled the island from the 9th to the 11th century. At that time, it was called *itriyya* ('long thin strands'), and was later adapted to *trie* ('thin strips'), and then *spaghetti*, meaning 'little strings'.

Above: Batches of spaghetti hanging up to dry in the 1930s

8

FROM THE PORT TO THE PANTRY

The Sicilian capital, Palermo, was a glittering Mediterranean port city under Arab rule. Enjoying a balmy microclimate, it was also a perfect place for Arab agronomists and horticulturalists to pioneer new scientific thinking in propagation, irrigation, crop rotation and companion planting (such as grapes alongside olives). Under their husbandry, food production increased and new crops were adapted to the Mediterranean ecosystem, including rice, sugarcane, citrus fruits and melons. Their technique of 'thinning' out the number of buds on a melon vine to produce a more intensely flavoured fruit (as demonstrated by the Sultan of Seville in the 11th century) is still used by Mantua's celebrated melon producer Zerbinati.

Palermo's template of a thriving port city served by a wide-ranging trade network was to be repeated around the Italian peninsula in the ports of Amalfi, Pisa, Genoa, Venice and Ancona. These became the great maritime republics of the Middle Ages, with each city dominating certain trade routes and holding overseas colonies in the Adriatic, Aegean, Near East and North Africa. Venice's *contado* (dependent countryside) was

SUGAR & SPICES

By the time Marco Polo returned home from China in 1299, Venice's Rialto was the most important wholesale market in the world. Sugar and spices became a European addiction and the use of saffron, nutmeg, cloves, cardamom and pepper widespread, giving us sweet-and-sour dishes such as agnoli *(ravioli stuffed with capon, cinnamon and cloves),* sbrisolona *(a hard biscuit with almonds) and* mostarda *(candied fruit and mustard relish).*

virtually the whole of the upper Adriatic, including vast tracts of land in Istria, Dalmatia and Greece.

With the rise of Venice's mercantile empire, northern Italy was at the vanguard of Europe's transformation from an agricultural society to a medieval powerhouse of trade. As Venetian and Genoese seamen offloaded expensive cargoes from around the Mediterranean, tradesmen distributed them via Italy's longest navigable river, the Po, to cities including Turin, Pavia, Milan, Piacenza, Parma, Mantua, Ferrara, Verona, Vicenza and Padua. It was in this connected, commercial environment that Italy's great cuisine was born.

COOKING IN THE RENAISSANCE

The Renaissance was a period of culinary creativity. Powerful clans such as the della Scala family in Verona, the Sforzas in Milan, the Medicis in Florence and the papacy in Rome derived power and wealth from taxing trade and the produce grown in the surrounding landscape, while also accumulating land through marriage alliances.

Opulent banquets became proxy displays of political power, where food was combined with theatre, music and dance. Leonardo da Vinci designed sets for the wedding banquet of Milan's Gian Galeazzo Sforza and Isabella of Aragon in 1489. Cristoforo da Messisbugo's 1548 book, *Banquets*, gives some idea of their scale and extravagance: a record of the wedding feast of the Duke of Ferrara's son Ercole II d'Este to Renée, the daughter of Louis XII of France, offers an endless list of courses, gifts and entertainments.

Below-stairs political manoeuvring was also underway as cooks brokered new relationships with possible patrons and suppliers, and made the effort to find new ingredients and recipes in order to keep up with the changing seasons and the fancies of their employers. Good cooks were in high demand, particularly ones like Martino de Rossi, who might be considered the Western world's first celebrity chef. His book *Libro de Arte Coquinaria* (The Art of Cooking; 1465) was a landmark of Italian gastronomic literature.

OPULENT BANQUETS BECOME PROXY DISPLAYS OF POLITICAL POWER

FOREIGN INFLUENCES

Between the 1600s and the 1800s, foreign influences brought new flavours to the Italian kitchen and spices went out of fashion. The French love of butter, cream, cheese and chocolate took hold in the northwest – particularly in Piedmont, which was controlled by the House of Savoy between 1416 and 1860. From across the Alps came tourists on the Grand Tour, French recipe books and the fashion for eating *a la russe* (Russian style), in separate courses comprising individual plates.

In Milan and the northwest, the Austrians introduced a penchant for sausages, cutlets and schnitzel: in Trieste, they still eat *jota* (sauerkraut soup) and sprinkle hunks of pork with *kren* (horseradish). With these new cultural and political ideas came new places to meet and eat. Cafés – serving Austrian *ciambella* and *castagnole* doughnuts and a new drink, coffee – were hothouses of political debate across the north, while the rise of the restaurant democratised access to good food.

A new, centralised bureaucracy and a reformed tax system increased Italy's agricultural output, while new crops revolutionised the diet of the masses. Potatoes, tomatoes, chillies and maize from colonies in the New World reached Spanish-controlled Naples in the 18th century, and a whole industry developed here around preserving tomatoes by bottling, juicing or concentrating them. Pizza was also invented in the Bourbon court, and in 1889 *pizzaiolo* (pizza-maker) Raffaele Esposito created the national pizza in honour of Queen Margherita of Savoy.

The most famous chef of the era and a cook at the Neapolitan court, gastronome Vincenzo Corrado coined the term 'Mediterranean cuisine' in his bestselling book *Il Cuoco Galante* (The Gallant Cook; 1773), which sang the praises of a largely vegetarian diet and advocated preparing and dressing food simply to allow natural flavours to shine. So healthy was this diet that, centuries later, the American physiologist Ancel Keys (who developed the US Army's K-rations during WWII) based his groundbreaking hypothesis that saturated fats cause heart disease on research conducted in Naples in the 1950s, and subsequently promoted the Mediterranean diet as the route to good health and longevity.

Above: A pizza seller in Naples, 1825

Venditore di pizze

11

Left: An Italian family dine on their terrace in 1950
Right: A 1930s advert for tomato puree

HOME COOKING

Until the early 20th century, the only Italian cookery books in circulation were written by men: chefs, stewards and courtiers working in the wealthiest city households with the finest ingredients. *Cucina casalinga* (home cooking) had no place at this elite table until the 1920s and '30s, when the impact of two world wars and the deprivations of the Depression saw middle-class housewives pushed out of the kitchen and into the workplace, where some found their way into print.

The first Italian cookery book written by a woman was *Come Posso Mangiar Bene?* (How Can I Eat Well?), written by home-cook Giulia Tamburini and published in 1900. Tamburini was the first in a long line of northern Italian housewives – including, most recently, Anna del Conte, whose *Risotto with Nettles*

recalls her wartime Milanese childhood and its influence on her cooking – who valued good food but, by necessity, had to work within a limited budget.

Thanks to them, a simple, filling *primo* (first course) of *minestra* (soup), gnocchi, risotto or pasta now sits at the heart of the Italian meal. Whether in the form of make-do classics such as *mondeghili* (Milanese meatballs made with leftover meat), *minestrone* (a rich vegetable soup fortified with rice and pancetta) or *pasta rasa* (egg pasta cooked in a broth with tomatoes, beans, potatoes, onions and garlic), the *primo* allowed middle-class families to live with a modicum of comfort. The more expensive second course of fish or meat was a secondary concern: liver or butter-fried eggs during the week, roast chicken or veal cutlets on Sundays.

AN INDUSTRIOUS KITCHEN

It's remarkable that despite recent industrialisation and radical food-related changes (the country's first supermarket opened in Milan in 1957, and its first fast-food outlet in 1982), the food on Italian tables remains largely local, seasonal and artisanal. Italians buy just a quarter of the frozen products sold in Britain, and 50% of their spending is still on fresh, unpackaged goods. Just check out the food markets in Milan, Rome, Naples and Palermo to witness the health of the local food economy.

There are over 70,000 regis-tered agribusinesses in Lombardy alone, producing 15% of Italy's food and, together with Piedmont, 30% of Europe's rice crop. Many of these industrial-scale products are actually some of the country's most genuine: ham, cheese, salami, pasta and rice were designed for preservation, transport and trade. Northern Italy's agribusinesses include 25% of the country's DOP and IGP quality-assured meat and cheese products, and 60% of its quality-assured wines. What's more, in December 2018, the FSI (Food Sustainability Index) announced Italy as a world leader in organics, sustainable agriculture and biodiversity preservation.

TIPICITA

Tipicita, *or typicality, describes the magical aura that food acquires when local identity is invested in it. In Italian, tipico has become synonymous with* buono: *something good, wholesome and delicious.*

SLOW FOOD PIONEERS

Combine culinary passion with commitment to artisan produce: the result is Slow Food, an Italian movement which has taken the world by storm.

The year is 1987. McDonald's has just begun expansion into Italy with the opening of its largest outlet to date, in the heart of Rome. Enter Carlo Petrini and a handful of other journalists from small-town Bra, Piedmont. Determined to buck the trend, these *neoforchettoni* ('big forks', or foodies) did more than just join anti fast-food protests – they created a manifesto. Published in the like-minded culinary magazine *Gambero Rosso*, it declared that a meal should be judged not by its speed, but by its pleasure.

The organisation they founded became known worldwide as Slow Food (www.slowfood.com), and its mission to reconnect artisanal producers with enthusiastic, educated consumers has taken root: there are now around 100,000 members in over 160 countries – not to mention Slow Food agriturismos (farm-stay accommodation), restaurants, farms, wineries, cheesemakers and revitalised farmers markets across Italy.

In addition, Slow Food's Ark of Taste catalogue aims to protect and promote indigenous edibles and ancient farming and food production methods which are threatened by industrialisation, globalisation and environmental degradation. Administered from headquarters in Florence, the list includes famous Tuscan products such as *lardo di colonnata* (marble-cured salami), *farro* (spelt), Chianina beef and Cinta Senese, the indigenous Tuscan pig.

While the main objective of the Slow Food movement is to protect local, traditional foods from the negative impacts of consumerism, of which fast food is symptomatic, there is an increasingly important health aspect, too. A WHO report released in May 2018 showed that Italy's childhood obesity rate had skyrocketed, with 21% of boys and 14% of girls now classified as obese. By promoting properly grown, sustainable food and Italy's famous Mediterranean diet, Slow Food hopes to reconnect people with responsible food culture and healthy eating habits.

14

THE SLOW FOOD CALENDAR

Italy's top Slow Food event is the biennial Terra Madre Salone del Gusto (www.salonedelgusto.com), held in Turin in even-ended years. It features Slow Food producers, chefs, activists, restaurateurs, farmers, scholars, environmentalists and epicureans from around the world...not to mention the world's best finger food. In odd-ended years, special events include Slow Fish (http://slowfish.slowfood.it) in Genoa and Cheese (www.cheese.slowfood.it) in Bra.

EATALY TORINO LINGOTTO
The original Slow Food mothership houses a staggering array of sustainable food and drink in a converted factory.

EATALY MILANO SMERALDO
Located in an old theatre, it's worth a visit to dine at Viviana Varese's Michelin-starred restaurant, Alice.

FICO EATALY WORLD BOLOGNA
The largest gastronomic theme park in the world, featuring 45 restaurants as well as workshops and demonstrations.

EATALY BARI
Located close to Bari's excellent fish market, with a waterside restaurant serving local fish dishes.

MEALS

'Tutti a tavola!' ('Everyone to the
table!') is a command every Italian
heeds. Traffic lights might be mere
suggestions and queues a fine idea in
theory, but to arrive late at the table
is unthinkable in Italy.

MORNING ESSENTIALS

In Italy, *colazione*
(breakfast) is a minimalist
affair. Eggs, pancakes,
ham, sausages, toast
and orange juice are
only likely to appear
at weekend *'brrrunch'*
(pronounced with the
rolled Italian 'r'), an
American import popular
only at trendy urban
eateries in big cities.

Italy's breakfast staple
is *caffè* (coffee). Espresso,
cappuccino (espresso
with a goodly dollop of
foamed milk) or *caffè
latte* – the hot, milky
espresso beverage that
Starbucks mistakenly
shortened to *latte*, which
will get you a glass of milk
in Italy. An alternative
is *orzo*, a slightly
nutty, non-caffeinated
roasted-barley beverage
that looks like cocoa.
It's a good substitute in
situations where decaf
(*deca*) isn't available.

With a *tazza* (cup)
in one hand, use the
other for the Italian
breakfast food of choice
– a pastry. Especially
promising options
include the following:

CORNETTO

The Italian take on the
French croissant is
usually smaller, lighter,
less buttery and slightly
sweet, with an orange-
rind glaze brushed on
top. Options might
include *semplice* (plain),
integrale (wholewheat),
cioccolato (chocolate),
crema (custard) or
varying flavours of
marmellata (jam).

CROSTATA

This breakfast tart with
a dense, buttery crust is
filled with your choice
of fruit jam, perhaps
amarena (sour cherry),
albicocca (apricot) or
frutti di bosco (wild berry).

DOUGHNUTS

Chow down on a
ciambella (also called
by its German name,
krapfen), the classic
fried-dough treat rolled
in granulated sugar and
sometimes filled with jam
or custard. Join the line
at kiosks and street fairs
for *fritole*, fried dough
studded with golden
raisins and sprinkled with
confectioners' sugar;
and *zeppole* (also called
bignè di San Giuseppe),
chewy doughnuts filled
with ricotta or *zucca*
(pumpkin), rolled in
confectioners' sugar and
handed over in a paper
cone to be devoured
dangerously hot.

VIENNOISERIE

The colonisation of
Northern Italy by the
Austro-Hungarian
Empire in the 19th
century had its upside: a
vast selection of sweet
buns and other rich
baked goods. Standouts
include cream-filled
brioches and *strudel di
mele*, an Italian adap-
tation of the traditional
Viennese apple strudel.

SUNDAY LUNCH is sacred EVERYWHERE

PRANZO (LUNCH)

Italian food culture directly contradicts what we think we know of Italy. A nation prone to perpetual motion in its Vespas, Ferraris and Bianchi bikes always pauses for *pranzo* (lunch) – hence the term *la pausa* ('the pause') to describe the midday break. In the cities, power-lunchers settle in at their favourite restaurants (*ristoranti*) and trattorias (*trattorie*) at 12.30–1pm, while in smaller towns and villages workers often head home for a two- to three-hour midday break, devouring a hot lunch and resting up before returning to work fortified by espresso. Sunday lunch is sacred everywhere.

Where *la pausa* has been scaled back to a scandalous hour and a half – barely enough time to get through the lines at the bank and bolt some *pizza al taglio* (pizza by the slice) – *rosticcerie* (rotisseries) or *tavole calde* (literally 'hot tables') keep the harried sated with steamy on-the-go options like roast chicken or *supplì* (fried risotto balls with a molten mozzarella centre). Bakeries and bars are also on hand with focaccia, panini and *tramezzini* (triangular stacked sandwiches made with squishy white bread).

18

APERITIVO & APERICENA

Aperitivo is often described as a 'pre-meal drink and light snacks'. Don't be fooled. Italian happy hour can easily turn into a budget-friendly dinner disguised as a casual drink (otherwise known as apericena). Some aperitivo cocktails are accompanied by a buffet of antipasti, pasta salads, cold cuts and some hot dishes (which may include your fellow diners – aperitivi is prime time for singles on the hunt).

You can methodically pillage buffets in cities like Milan, Turin, Rome, Florence, Naples and Palermo from 5pm or 6pm to around 8pm or 9pm for the price of a single drink – which crafty diners nurse for the duration. Venetians, however, enjoy their own unique version of aperitivo: an ombra (a half-glass of wine) and bargain sea-food cicheti (Venetian tapas).

Italy's aperitivo culture originates in Turin, where Antonio Benedetto Carpano infused Moscato white wine with herbs and spices to create Vermouth in 1786. The drink quickly gained a reputation for piquing the appetite, turning the bar in which Carpano worked into Turin's pre-dinner hotspot. These days, a favourite aperitivo libation is the spritz, a mix of prosecco, soda water and either Aperol, Campari or the more herbacious Cynar. Not surprisingly, aperitivi are wildly popular among the many young Italians who can't afford to eat dinner out, but still want a place to enjoy food while schmoozing with friends – leave it to Italy to find a way to put the glamour into budget drinking and dining.

CENA (DINNER)

Traditionally, cena (dinner) is lunch's lighter sibling and cries of 'Oh, I can hardly eat anything tonight' are still common after a marathon weekend lunch. 'Maybe just a bowl of pasta, a salad, some cheese and fruit...' Don't be fooled: even if you've been invited to someone's house for a 'light dinner', wine and elastic-waisted trousers are always advisable.

But while your Italian hosts may insist you devour one more ricotta-filled cannolo ('surely you don't have them back home...and even if you did, surely they're not as good?'), your friendly restaurant waiter will usually show more mercy.

A full-blown Italian meal in a restaurant usually consists of an antipasto (starter), a primo piatto (first course), a secondo piatto (second course) with an insalata (salad) or contorno (vegetable side dish), dolci (sweet), plus fruit, coffee and digestivo (liqueur). Few Italians eat meals this large, though. When eating out, you can follow the example of most Italians and mix and match.

From top: Market stalls in Rome's Campo de' Fiori; Bread gnocchi with black olive pesto and pecorino; At mealtimes, Italy takes a pause from its perpetual motion

Left: Dining is an intrinsic part of Italian culture

ETIQUETTE

Eating is a serious business in Italy, and dining out or at some-one's home is considered an event. When your host furnishes you with an attractive setting, carefully sourced produce and a well-planned menu of lovingly prepared dishes, you are required to play your part too.

This means dressing appropriately (restaurants deserve a bit of glamour, while smart casual clothes are fine for *osterie* and *trattorie*). Turning up in sweaty beachwear, scruffy T-shirts (particularly at dinner) or in a generally unkempt state is an insult to your host and may make finding a table in fashionable or popular places hard. In contrast, if you're sporting a fine *bella figura* (literally 'beautiful figure'), the maitre d' will probably go the extra mile to squeeze you in – because beautiful diners make for beautiful restaurants.

Likewise, good manners and social graces are much appreci-ated. With millions of travellers visiting annually and demanding to be fed daily, service in some Italian restaurants and tourist hotspots can be slow, harried or indifferent, particularly if you arrive unannounced without a booking and expect unusual or unseasonal items. Booking ahead (you can usually ask your hotel to do this) is always appreciated in busy restaurants. Or, simply apologise that you were unable to make a reservation and ask politely if they can fit you in. They usually will.

DiNiNG OUT

When you sit down, you'll be asked if you want fizzy or still water. If you prefer you can ask for tap water (*acqua del rubinetto*), which is perfectly potable all across Italy. Bread will also arrive. It is served without butter (olive oil may be offered instead) and without side plates. It's fine to put it on the table.

When perusing the menu and ordering, feel free to tap into your server's knowledge of seasonal produce or daily specials – you'll notice Italian diners conversing at length about dishes. Solicit your server's advice, pick two options that sound interesting, and ask them to recommend one over the other. When that's done, snap the menu shut and say *'Allora, facciamo cosi, per favore!'* ('Well then, let's do that, please!'). You have just won over your server, and flattered the chef – promising omens for a memorable meal to come.

While you don't have to order the full four- or five-course menu, it's usual to have an *antipasto* (starter) to get things going while your next course – either a *primo* (pasta course) or *secondo* (main of meat or fish) – is being prepared. *Antipasto* plates of charcuterie or cheese are typically large and meant for sharing. For lunch in a trattoria, it's fine to order a single course: a simple bowl of pasta, soup or plate of charcuterie.

Fine meals always call for wine, often available by the glass or carafe. There's no need to avoid house wines, as they are usually good local labels and no self-respecting Italian would serve (or drink) bad wine. As Italy has such a diversity of varieties and producers, you're unlikely to recognise many of the names on the wine list. Again, don't be shy about asking servers for advice – they are often very pleased to explain unusual local offerings. Make eye contact when toasting (*'cin cin!'*), but never clink using plastic cups: it's bad luck!

When you finally get down to eating, take a moment to appreciate the look of and aroma rising from your plate. Wish other diners *'buon appetito'* ('good appetite') and tuck in. If you're eating spaghetti or long pasta, twirl it around your fork (no spoons, please, its rude) and bite through hanging strands rather than slurping. Eating bread with your pasta is considered *'un po' strano'* ('a bit strange'), though using it to wipe any remaining sauce from your plate is fine. Feel free to give your *'complimenti allo chef'* ('compliments to the chef') or a simple, satisfied *'delizioso'* ('delicious') when your server removes your plate.

Dessert, usually a simple panna cotta, tiramisu or ice-cream, is often skipped in favour of a coffee. Italians don't drink cappuccino after 11am, and certainly not after a meal, when an espresso is the only respectable choice (with, perhaps, a *digestivo*).

On the subject of *il conto* (the bill), whoever invites usually pays. Splitting the bill is common enough, though itemising it is very vulgar (*'molto vulgare'*). If there is no *servizio* (service charge), consider leaving a 10% to 15% tip.

Right: A family-run restaurant in the Valle d'Aosta, Northwest Italy

DINING AT AN ITALIAN HOME

You've heard that old myth about the Italian mamma who keeps feeding you until you're just about to burst? It's not a myth. An abundance of food on a table is a sign of hospitality, and you refuse it at your peril. Likewise, if you are invited to someone's home, don't turn up empty handed. Take a tray of *dolci* (sweets) from a *pasticceria* (pastry shop) as a gift.

Hungry guests with hearty appetites are the most welcome. And an enthusiastic interest in and enjoyment of the food on the table is much appreciated. Older Italians may even show genuine concern for those who are noticeably thin. This isn't some outdated stereotype, but a reminder that in the not-too-distant past many less affluent Italians had very little to eat.

Table settings will be the same as at most restaurants. There will be two forks and one knife (and a spoon, if you're eating soup). You won't be given a bread plate and it's normal to break the bread over the cloth and lay it there while you eat. There may well be just one glass for both water and wine; you drink a glass of one, followed by a glass of the other.

There will certainly be more than one course. Many families will bring out the prosciutto to carve at the table. *Salumi* (cold cuts), often homemade, will be sliced and offered, a great steaming bowl of pasta or risotto is a certainty, then comes a small serving of meat or fish, and, finally, salad and fruit. Big meals may also include a soup, a second pasta course, a sweet, or all three. You should place your knife and fork back on the table after each course until after the salad or vegetable. If there are two forks, the first can be left in your emptied pasta bowl to be cleared.

As you're finishing your pasta you should *fare la scarpetta* ('make a shoe') with your bread and wipe your plate clean – a sign you really enjoyed the meal and one that won't go unnoticed. Bones from things like cutlets can be handled with the fingers (and fingers can be surreptitiously licked) and accompanied by small appreciative exclamations of enjoyment, which are positively welcomed. Avoid eating with your mouth open, or talking with your mouth full. Serviettes aren't generally tucked into collars while eating pasta.

BUSINESS MEALS

The business lunch is not only alive and well in Italy, it's an art form. Taking clients out for a meal is not just considered a friendly gesture, it is an important act of hospitality and a sign of respect. What's more, the meal you're invited to is just that, an enjoyable social meal. It isn't an opportunity for a hard-sell or for further business discussion.

The venue will usually be selected for the quality of the food rather than how fancy or upmarket a restaurant is: the aim is probably to show off the very best regional or local specialities. Prepare yourself to indulge in numerous courses – rushing through one or two just wouldn't be a good show of hospitality.

Finally, whoever invites pays – any offers of a contribution will be firmly rejected. Simply show your appreciation by complimenting the food and your host's excellent choice of restaurant.

DATING

If someone you've met has turned your head, you may invite them for an initial coffee ('offro caffè?') or, even better, an ice-cream. If things progress well you can then move on to an *aperitivo* – an early evening spritz or cocktail which will be delivered with a supply of small snacks and which can be stretched out for several hours if a date is going well. Otherwise, your best bet is to invite your prospective date out for pizza – the country's best-loved and most affordable food staple. In larger cities, such as Milan, Rome and Florence, it is becoming more common to split the bill, but elsewhere in Italy, men typically pay.

PICNICKING

Think twice before you plop yourself down on church steps or in the middle of a historic piazza to grab a quick *panino* (sandwich) or other takeaway lunch – it is forbidden in an increasing number of historic Italian cities such as Rome, Florence and Venice, and hefty fines can be legally levied. Look for the nearest bench or city park – and always dispose of rubbish in the nearest bin or take it with you.

Clockwise from left:
Diners in a Venice sidestreet; A traditional picnic spread; Places are set in a Lombardy restaurant; Veal *saltimbocca* with carrot mash

FESTIVALS

Perhaps you've heard of ancient Roman orgies with trips to the *vomitorium* to make room for the next course, or of Medici family feasts with sugar sculptures worth their weight in gold? In Italy, culinary indulgence is the centre of any celebration, and major holidays are defined by their specialities.

GIORNO DI MAGRO

The classic way to celebrate any feast day in Italy is to precede it with a day of eating *magro* (lean) to prepare for the overindulgence to come. On Vigilia (Christmas Eve), for example, tradition dictates that you eat little during the day and have a fish-based dinner as a prelude to the excesses of 25 December.

CARNIVALE

The first major celebration of the year is *Carnevale* (Carnival) before the commencement of Lent. It is a time for *migliaccio di polenta* (a casserole of polenta, sausages, and pecorino and parmesan cheeses), *sanguinaccio* ('blood pudding' made with dark chocolate and cinnamon), *chiacchiere* (fried biscuits sprinkled with icing sugar) and Sicily's *mpagnuccata* (deep-fried dough tossed in soft caramel).

From left: *Zeppole* with cinnamon and sugar; Celebrating Easter with a marzipan lamb; Panettone; Truffles

ST JOSEPH'S DAY

Hot on the heels of *Carnevale*, on 19 March, is St Joseph's Feast Day. Expect to eat *bignè di San Giuseppe* (fried doughnuts filled with cream or chocolate) in Rome; *zeppole* (fritters topped with lemon-scented cream, sour cherry and dusting sugar) in Naples and Bari; and *crispelle di riso* (citrus-scented rice fritters dipped in honey) in Sicily.

EASTER

Lent specialities like Sicilian *quaresimali* (almond biscuits) give way to Easter bingeing with the obligatory lamb and *colomba* (dove-shaped cake). Egg reigns supreme in regional specialities like Genoa's *torta pasqualina* (tart with ricotta, parmesan, artichokes and hard-boiled eggs), Florence's *brodetto* (egg, lemon and bread broth) and Naples' legendary *pastiera* (shortcrust pastry tart with ricotta, cream, candied fruits and cereals, flavoured with orange water).

CHRISTMAS

Christmas means stuffed pasta, seafood dishes and one of Milan's greatest inventions: *panettone* (a golden sweet bread studded with raisins and dried fruit). Further south, Neapolitans gorge on *raffioli* (sponge and marzipan biscuits) and *struffoli* (tiny fried pastry balls dipped in honey and sprinkled with colourful candied sugar and marzipan), while their Sicilian cousins toast the season with *cucciddatu* (ring-shaped cakes made with dried figs, nuts, honey, vanilla, cloves, cinnamon and citrus fruits).

SAGRE

Of course, it's not all about religion. Some Italian holidays dispense with the spiritual premise and are just a pure celebration of local food products. During spring, summer and early autumn, towns across Italy celebrate *sagre*, festivals dedicated to seasonal foods. You'll find a *sagra del tartufo* (truffles) in Umbria, del *pomodoro* (tomatoes) in Sicily and *del cipolle* (onions) in Puglia. For a list of *sagre*, check out www.paesidelgusto.it (in Italian).

food festival
CALENDAR

Italy's *sagre* are one of the country's most enjoyable and authentic food experiences. They exemplify the Italian approach to food as an event, a social occasion and moment to stop and enjoy life.

MAY

SAGRA DEL PESCE
Held to coincide with the feast of St Fortunato, patron saint of fishermen, vivacious fish festivals take place along the Italian Riviera in the towns of Rapallo, Camogli, Santa Margherita and chic Portofino.

PORCHETTIAMO
This succulent, slow-roast pork beloved of central Italy is celebrated in epic style over three days in the Umbrian town of San Terenziano di Gualdo Cattaneo.

GIROTONNO
Held on the tiny island of Carloforte off the coast of Sardinia, with its ancient tuna factory, this festival celebrates the deep tradition of tuna fishing.

SAGRA DELLE FRAGOLE (MAY/JUNE)
The small town of Nemi near Rome is famous for its *fragolino di bosco* (wild strawberries), which grow nearby in the sacred Nemus woodland. They're harvested in May, and related celebrations stretch through June.

JULY

SAGRA DEL CUOPPO
A celebration of Campania's most famous street food, the *cuoppo*, a paper cone filled with fried fish and veggies, or sweet *zeppole* (deep-fried sugared dough balls).

AUGUST

FÉHTA DOU LAR
The Aostan town of Arnad celebrates lard in a setting of wooden chalets decorated with flowers. Lard is the focus but regional cheese, wine and cakes are also on display.

SEPTEMBER

SAGRA NAZIONALE DEL GORGONZOLA
Visit the home of one of Italy's oldest and greatest cheeses, Gorgonzola, for a feast of cheesy treats.

FIERA DEL RISO
Italy's largest rice festival is held in the town of Isola della Scala, near Verona. On show are risottos and rice-based products, including *grappa*.

SAGRA DEL TORTELLINO TRADIZIONALE
The historic town of Castelfranco Emilia puts on demonstrations of

Left: A performance at Alba's white truffle fair

OCTOBER

NOVEMBER

sfogline (housewives) making central Italy's famous *tortellini* pasta.

COUS COUS FEST
Celebrating Arab influences in Sicilian cuisine, this festival invites African and Middle Eastern chefs to the town of San Vito Lo Capo for 10 days of cooking demonstrations and talks.

SAGRA DEL PEPERONCINO
Calabria's chilli pepper is best showcased in the town of Diamante, with a Championship of Chilli Eaters and a Spicy Cinema.

SAGRA DELL'UVA
Wine festivals crop up in harvest season all over Italy, but in the town of Marino, just south of Rome, even the central fountain flows with wine.

MORTADELLABÒ
Bologna's Mortadella festival is a celebration of Bolognese culture and of the first Italian food product given protected status; street-food stalls serve up thin slices with glasses of fizz.

INTERNATIONAL WHITE TRUFFLE FAIR
Alba's white truffle fair is world famous and fills the town with market stalls selling piles of truffles and all manner of related products.

FIERA NAZIONALE DEL MARRONE
The mountain town of Cuneo in Piedmont celebrates the sweeter cousin of the chestnut, *marrone*, in one of Italy's most popular annual food festivals.

BACCO NELLE GNOSTRE
A unique food festival held in Bari and Taranto, in which locals prepare food at home and share it with passers-by in *gnostre*, semi-private courtyards typical of the historic centres of both towns.

FESTA DEL TORRONE
Cremona's nougat festival is a pre-Christmas treat, with the 600-year-old sweet celebrated in style via all manner of food tastings and fireworks.

WHERE & HOW TO EAT

Italian dining culture is famous the world over, but it is much more than checked tablecloths and raffia-wrapped wine bottles covered in candle wax. Italians are passionate consumers of life's pleasures, food being chief among them, but they are also creatures of habit and tradition.

Left: Osteria
Bancogiro, Venice

Eating out in Italy is part of everyday life. While fancy restaurants tend to be reserved for formal or celebratory occasions, most Italians will pop out for one of the following during the day: breakfast, mid-morning coffee, a lunchtime sandwich, afternoon snack, *aperitivo* or pizza. These round-the-clock eating and drinking opportunities provide essential moments to catch up with neighbours, network with colleagues and socialise with friends, cementing the warm community ties that Italians so enjoy.

During the week, most Italians rise early and make a run for their neighbourhood bar to bolt down a coffee and pastry. Workers may pop out for a mid-morning snack or espresso, before lunch around 12.30-1pm. Most restaurants then close for a couple of hours, before reopening at 7-7.30pm, although most tables won't fill up until 8pm or 9pm. The further south you go in the summer, the later the dining hour, with some southern Italians sitting down at the table around 10pm in the height of summer. Inversely, in the north in winter, the dining hour may be as early as 7pm.

A typical Italian menu is divided into four, maybe five

courses. If this multi-course marathon sounds like too much, don't worry. Italians usually only indulge in epic meals on special occasions or Sunday lunch when they have hours to enjoy them. For daily dining, Italians have perfected the art of gourmet snacking, enjoying top-quality pastries with coffee, a thick sandwich stuffed with seasonal produce from a neighbourhood deli, an artisanal gelato or a glass of local wine with savoury bites at *aperitivo*.

For everyday meals in a trattoria they order as they like, even a single bowl of pasta with a glass of wine. You should follow suit. Then, relax. The food will arrive at a leisurely pace because bringing things too

EATING GREETINGS

On entering any bar or restaurant greet your hosts with a cordial buongiorno *(good morning)* or buonasera *(good evening). In busy bars or cafes you may have to pay for what you want at the cash register before taking your receipt to the bar and placing your order. In a restaurant, once you're seated, the first question your waiter will ask is* "cosa vuole da bere?", *which means "what would you like to drink?" Bread will arrive automatically.*

fast before you've had a chance to settle in is considered rude. In Italy, hospitality is key and it is unthinkable to rush diners through a meal so you can turn over tables.

Also, don't expect your waiter to hover over you asking how things are or topping up your water. Once he's advised you on the menu and specials, taken your order and brought you bread, water and wine, he'll leave you to enjoy your meal. If you want something from him, you'll need to catch his attention. You also won't receive your bill until you ask for it, because lingering at the table is part of the experience. After all, you're paying for dinner, not a drive-through!

The bill when it comes will include a nominal, mandatory cover charge, *pane e coperto* (literally, 'bread and cover'). In addition to this, most restaurants include a service (*servizio*) charge. If not, a couple of euros is fine in a pizzeria or trattoria, and 5-10% is usual in nice restaurants. Smoking is banned in all enclosed spaces, including restaurants and bars.

BiLL SPLiTTiNG

When your bill arrives, don't expect to split it seven ways. Although restaurants in large cities might be prepared to split the bill, most Italian restaurants won't as fees for charging credit and debit cards are high and multiple transactions costly. So, if you'd like to split the bill, try to pay with cash. In rural places, small restaurants may not take cards at all.

PLACES TO EAT

Take your pick according to your mood and your pocket – from the frenetic energy of pizzerias to warm third-generation-run trattorias, from chic bars laden with *apertivi* banquets to modern *osterie* restaurants.

While the Italian dining scene has become increasingly sophisticated over the last few decades, incorporating new food trends such as food trucks and raw bars, the family-run trattoria is still the country's most popular eatery. Traditional dining habits also remain strong, and different venues retain clearly defined roles. The only thing to remember is: don't judge a restaurant by its decor. Brilliant food can be served anywhere in Italy.

AGRITURISMO

An agriturismo is a working farm offering accommodation, as well as food made with farm-grown produce (some serve meals for lodgers only). They are generally very reasonably priced and rustic, serving typical local food that the farmer's wife has been cooking for her family for years. Most are open only for dinner and weekend lunches.

BAR/CAFFÈ

The Italian bar/caffè is a wonderful institution, open all day long (usually from 7.30am to 10pm), serving breakfast pastries, lunchtime sandwiches, *spuntini* (snacks) and *aperitivi* alongside coffee, soft drinks, basic cocktails and wine. When ordering at a busy bar, do so at the till (*cassa*), then take your receipt and repeat your order to the barman. If the bar is quiet and/or you are known there, the barman make take your order and you pay at the end. There is no hard and fast rule on this – just watch what the locals do.

BIRRERIA

Usually seen in the north of the country, a *birreria* is a bar that specialises in selling beer (usually local labels) alongside the usual café offerings. In the far north, don't be surprised to see someone leaning on the bar and drinking a beer for breakfast.

BRACERIA

A 'grill' serving a meat-focused menu, often with a counter displaying different cuts of meat. The selected portion is then cooked to order on an open grill. In the south, many *bracerie* adjoin the local butcher's shop. A *rosticceria* (roastery) is a similar concept, but serves roasted meat instead and also offers the ubiquitous roast-chicken takeaway.

ENOTECA

Italians rarely drink without eating, and you can eat well at many *enoteche*, wine bars that usually serve snacks such as *bruschette* (grilled bread topped with tomatoes), *crostini* (toasts with toppings) and platters of cheeses or cold meats, salads and a few simple hot dishes.

GELATERIA

Eating *gelato* is as much a part of Italian life as morning coffee – in Sicily, ice-cream in a brioche bun is a favourite breakfast snack. In artisanal *gelaterie*, flavours are strictly seasonal and ingredients sourced from the best locations (pistachios from Bronte, chocolate from Turin etc). In summer, *sorbetti* (sorbet) and *grattachecca* (literally 'scratched ice' topped with fruit and syrup) also hit the menu. Most *gelaterie* open from noon to 1am.

OSTERIA

In the past, *osterie* were family run places specialising in one dish and a *vino della casa* (house wine). Similar to a trattoria, their focus is on well-priced, traditional cooking. Modern *osterie* can be quite trendy, and usually sport short dinner-only menus featuring deceptively simple dishes based on regional ingredients.

PANINOTECA

With a rough translation as a bread roll (*panino*) place (*-teca*), this is a specialist sandwich shop. Even the simplest of fillings, for example prosciutto and pecorino, can be a joy to eat. Most *paninoteche* are open during normal daytime hours.

PASTICCERIA

Italian sweets and pastries have many influences. Pastry-making was a traditional pastime of nuns, who would sell their wares on festive occasions. The Sicilian sweet tooth is influenced by Middle Eastern flavours, while chocolate was brought to Sicily and Naples by the Spaniards. In the north, *pasticcerie* are modelled on French patisserie parlours and Austrian cake shops. *Pasticcerie* also double as cafés, with sweet and savoury pastry. Most open 7am–7pm.

SPAGHETTERIA

Spaghetterie are simple places that originated in the street-stalls of Naples, where punters could buy simple bowls of spaghetti with a choice of sauces. The name implies no-frills but generally delicious pasta and *secondi*, with correspondingly low prices. *Spaghetterie* are found predominantly in the south, but are less common these days.

TAVOLA CALDA

The old-school fast food venue, a *tavola calda* (literally 'hot table') serves inexpensive pre-prepared pasta, meat and vegetable dishes which you line up for, usually with a tray, cafeteria style. Most are open all day from about 11am.

PIZZERIA

Every Italian's favourite casual (and cheap) meal is a gloriously simple pizza with a bubbling topping. Most Italians precede their pizza with a starter of *bruschette* (grilled bread topped with vegetables, usually tomatoes) or *fritti* (mixed fried foods), and wash it down with beer. Pizzerias often only open in the evening, as their wood-fired ovens take a while to get going. For a snack on the run, *pizza al taglio* (pizza by the slice) places are open daily.

RISTORANTE

For Italians, restaurants represent fine dining venues with dressed tables, smart waiter service, sophisticated menus, comprehensive wine lists and correspondingly higher prices. Italians usually reserve restaurant dining for dates or special occasions rather than everyday meals.

TRATTORIA

Traditionally, trattorias are family run places that offer a basic, affordable local menu. The food is homemade and hearty and the service down-to-earth and amiable. Quality can vary in major tourist cities, but outside of these hotspots the cooking is usually reliably good. Trattorias generally open for both lunch and dinner.

MENUS

A typical Italian menu is divided into *antipasti* (appetisers), *primi* (pasta or soup first course), *secondi* (meat or fish second course) with *contorni* (vegetable side dishes), and *dolci* (dessert). Fine-dining restaurants may divide sections further into *terra* (land) and *mare* (sea) as, traditionally, it was considered unhealthy to eat mixed courses of meat and fish. There may also be daily specials. Consider ordering these: they are usually the freshest, most exciting items on the menu.

In some cheaper *trattorie* or *osterie*, particularly in rural areas and in the south of the country, there may be no menu at all – instead, your server will explain the day's dishes to you.

In tourist hotspots, some restaurants may offer a *menù turistico* (tourist menu). These typically feature hybrid Italian dishes such as spaghetti Bolognese (which doesn't exist in Italy). Their offerings aren't usually regional or seasonal – avoid them if possible.

All popular restaurants offer *vino della casa* (house wine) – it is generally good quality and great value. Wine can be drunk by the glass, as a *quartino* (quarter litre), carafe or by the bottle. In top-tier restaurants, you'll be handed a comprehensive wine list, often divided into local and foreign (*esteri*) wines.

TYPES OF MENU

MENÙ ALLA CARTA
Choose whatever you like from the menu.

MENÙ DI DEGUSTAZIONE
Degustation menu, usually consisting of six to eight 'tasting size' courses.

MENÙ TURISTICO
The 'tourist menu' usually signals mediocre fare for gullible tourists – steer clear!

MENÙ FISSO
An affordable fixed-price menu; quite rare in Italy and usually only found at lunchtime in popular *trattorie* frequented by working people.

Menu Decoder

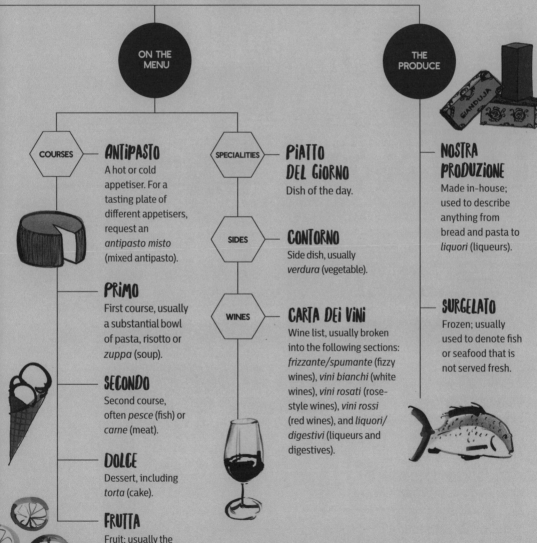

ON THE MENU

COURSES

ANTIPASTO
A hot or cold appetiser. For a tasting plate of different appetisers, request an *antipasto misto* (mixed antipasto).

PRIMO
First course, usually a substantial bowl of pasta, risotto or *zuppa* (soup).

SECONDO
Second course, often *pesce* (fish) or *carne* (meat).

DOLCE
Dessert, including *torta* (cake).

FRUTTA
Fruit; usually the epilogue to a meal.

SPECIALITIES

PIATTO DEL GIORNO
Dish of the day.

SIDES

CONTORNO
Side dish, usually *verdura* (vegetable).

WINES

CARTA DEI VINI
Wine list, usually broken into the following sections: *frizzante/spumante* (fizzy wines), *vini bianchi* (white wines), *vini rosati* (rose-style wines), *vini rossi* (red wines), and *liquori/ digestivi* (liqueurs and digestives).

THE PRODUCE

NOSTRA PRODUZIONE
Made in-house; used to describe anything from bread and pasta to *liquori* (liqueurs).

SURGELATO
Frozen; usually used to denote fish or seafood that is not served fresh.

COURSES

A full Italian meal consists of four or five courses. Few Italians eat meals this large, though, unless they are attending a special occasion, family gathering or a wedding. When eating out, you should do as most Italians do, and mix and match.

1

STUZZICHERIE

The name comes from *stuzzicare*, which means to 'whet the appetite', and describes a small snack or amuse-bouche to get things going. The term is only seen occasionally on menus, along with the more commonly used expression *spuntini*, meaning snacks.

2

ANTIPASTI

Literally translated as 'before the pasta', this is the appetiser which typically features all manner of seafood (oysters, crustaceans, marinated anchovies), *carpaccio* (raw seafood or meat), *bruschetta* (grilled bread with a variety of toppings), platters of *salumi* (small cured goods) such as prosciutto, salami or cheese, and fruit such as melon or figs with soft cheeses like mozzarella and burrata.

3

PRIMI

This is the heart of the Italian meal, the 'first' course. *Primi* are mostly pasta today. Traditionally, in the north of the country it would have been *minestre*, a bowl of vegetables, legumes, pasta or rice cooked in stock (minestrone is only one of many *minestra* soups); or risotto, rice cooked in stock with vegetables, meat or seafood. In Emilia-Romagna, the menu may include tortellini served in *brodo* (broth). Further south, pasta or *zuppa* (soup) are more typical. *Zuppa* is a broth made with soaked bread (never pasta or rice).

4

SECONDI

The 'second' course was traditionally a small portion of meat (*carne*) or fish (*pesce*), to follow the more filling first course. In cities, you'll likely get a choice of both meat and fish, but in traditional restaurants, the menu may only feature either fish if you're at the seaside or near a lake or river, or meat if you're in a mountainous region. Meat and fish *secondi* are served without any accompaniments; if you want vegetables you should order a *contorno* (side dish) or *insalata* (salad).

5

CONTORNI

Contorni are side-dishes, usually grilled seasonal vegetables or salads. Some of the most common include *patate al forno* (oven-baked potatoes), *spinaci* (spinach), *verdure miste* (mixed vegetables) and *insalata verde* (green salad). Vegetables are generally basted in olive oil, salted and chargrilled. Salads usually come undressed as the table is furnished with oil, vinegar and salt so you can opt to add to the leaves. Start with the vinegar – if you dress with the oil first, the vinegar won't coat the salad.

6

DOLCI/FRUTTA

Dolci (desserts) tend to be the same at every trattoria, and often in restaurants, too: tiramisu (made with *savoiardi* biscuits layered with a custard made from coffee, egg yolks, sugar, mascarpone and marsala wine); panna cotta ('cooked cream' with added sugar, cooled to set), *zabaglione* (rich custard made with egg yolks and a sweet wine) and *torta di nonna* ('grandma's cake'; sweet-crust tart with a custard and fruit filling). In the south of the country, where dairy products are less widely used, fruit is also a typical dessert.

VEGETARIAN & VEGAN DINING

Italian cooking distinguishes itself among European cuisines by virtue of its abundant use of vegetables.

Since the Middle Ages, Italian cooks have worked with a huge range of garden produce and aromatic herbs, and these continue to hold an important place on the Italian table.

As a result, vegetarians eat exceedingly well in Italy, with a wide choice of non-meat *antipasti*, soups, salads, pasta, bean- and grain-based dishes, *contorni* (side dishes) and pizzas. Although the Italian consumption of vegetables may originate in past poverty, over the centuries this habit has transformed into an essential element of the customs, skills and culture that define the national cuisine. In order to prepare an excellent salad here, it is not enough to just procure a range of fine greens – Italian cooks must also know how to treat the ingredients appropriately.

To many Italians, being vegetarian means you don't eat red meat. Few are strictly vegetarian, although many eat meat in limited quantities. Those who are particularly religious may only eat meat on certain days of the week according to liturgical rules of 'lean' (*magro*) and 'fat' (*grasso*) days; while those in the more impoverished, more rural, south of Italy naturally tend to consume more vegetables and grains in their diet.

USEFUL PHRASES

Io sono vegano/vegana
I am vegan (masculine/feminine)

Non mangio prodotti di origine animale
I don't eat animal products

Non mangio i latticini
I don't eat dairy products

Contiene uova?
Does it contain eggs?

Avete latte di soia?
Do you have soya milk?

Avete gelato senza latte?
Do you have gelato without milk?

42

From top: A chef prepares chicory and broad bean puree; A vegan pizza with an oat-rich base

In big cities such as Milan, Rome, Florence, Venice and Naples, there are increasing numbers of vegetarian, vegan and raw-food restaurants and cafés; Turin has even gone so far as to aspire to being Italy's first 'vegan city'. Nearly all high-end restaurants offer vegetarian choices, and modern bar-caffés and *pasticcerie* increasingly serve *cornetti vegani* (vegan croissants) and *latte di soia* (soya milk). Even vegan gelato is readily available in many big-city *gelaterie* (if you're ever not sure, opt for the equally excellent dairy-free sorbet instead).

On regular menus, be mindful of hidden ingredients in dishes that may sound vegetarian – for example, steer clear of anything that's been stuffed (like courgette flowers, often spiced up with anchovies) or pastas with tomato sauce which might be enriched with *guanciale* (pork jowl). To be sure, check that your dish is '*senza carne o pesce*' (without meat or fish).

Vegans are in for a tougher time due to the ubiquitous use of cheese. This is particularly true in the north of the country, where all things dairy (milk, cheese, yoghurt, butter) play a central role in the diet. For example, risotto may seem like a vegan-friendly dish, but it's often made with meat or fish stock, and usually includes cheese and butter. In the south, where the use of butter gives way to olive oil, menus are often more vegan-friendly.

Cheese is used universally, so you must specify that you want something '*senza formaggio*' (without cheese) when ordering food. Also remember that *pasta fresca* (fresh pasta), which may turn up in soups, is made with eggs. Virtually all *dolci* (sweets), including gelato, contain eggs, milk or both. The Happy Cow website and app (www.happycow.net) are useful resources for finding vegetarian and vegan restaurants in Italy.

ALLERGIES & INTO

The Mediterranean diet is based on a number of ingredients – durum wheat, milk, cheese, eggs, shellfish, tomatoes and nuts – that may be of concern to some travellers. Outside of main tourist areas, you'll need to keep your wits about you.

ALLERGIES

Awareness of food allergies in Italy is increasing, although sometimes not widely catered for. That said, food is such an intrinsic part of Italian culture and Italians want you to enjoy your meal.

EU laws specify that restaurant menus should label the top 14 allergens, including celery, cereals containing gluten, crustaceans, eggs, fish, lupin, milk, molluscs, mustard, nuts, peanuts, sesame seeds, soya and sulphites. This is done using letters: A signifies dishes including cereals containing gluten; C eggs; E peanuts; G milk and lactose etc. However, outside cities, few Italian menus include these.

If you have a food allergy, come prepared. People at risk of anaphylactic reaction should carry an autoinjector/ EpiPen (you need a medical prescription to obtain one in Italy) and an Allergy Card. Food Allergy Italia (www. foodallergyitalia.org) has created a 'Chef Card' that you can customise, along with templates in Italian explaining serious allergies and a note to use in case of an emergency. Keep a note of the emergency phone number: 118.

If you are allergic to milk or peanuts, avoid fried food because peanut oil is often used and/ or the same oil might be used to fry food with milk

protein. Likewise, avoid stuffed pasta, which often includes nuts or milk products. Pesto contains pine nuts and cheese; walnuts, hazelnuts, pistachios, chestnuts and almonds are widely used in all kinds of dishes; and mortadella may contain pistachio. Steer clear of

sauces, which may include hidden ingredients; and be careful of baked goods, which could be made with lupin flours and nuts; and chocolate, which is often mixed with hazelnuts. If eating gelato, be aware of possible cross-contamination from the scoop.

...ERANCES

INTOLERANCES

Wheat is in all the main staples of Italian food, from bread to pasta to pizza. If you're coeliac, check the Italian Celiac Association's website (www.celiachia.it); it's in Italian, but is fairly simple to navigate and enables you to search for restaurants, pizzerias and hotels that are familiar with coeliac disease and offer gluten-free food.

In large cities, numerous restaurants now offer gluten-free options. Just say *'Io sono celiaco'* or *'senza glutine'* when you sit down, and the waiters will usually be able to recommend suitable dishes. If there's no clear guidance on the menu, pick out a couple of simple dishes that might be okay and ask: *'È senza glutine?'* ('Is it gluten-free?').

If you are lactose-intolerant, you might find that you can eat some dairy items in Italy that you can't back home. That's because when cheeses are aged, the bacteria consume lactose. Most lactose is gone after three months of ageing and processed cheeses have more lactose than others. So, you might find you're fine with harder, aged cheeses, like parmesan or pecorino.

GLUTEN ALTERNATIVES

Gluten is the essential element that holds pasta together, and without it a pasta dough cannot be formed. Corn, which is used as an alternative, for example, contains no gluten, so artificial products are added to hold corn pasta together; these can be unhealthy in their own way, so always check the ingredients.

Tip sheet

Carry an autoinjector/EpiPen with you whenever eating out

Read or ask about the ingredients before ordering a dish

Carry an Allergy Card or bring a note explaining your food allergies

Inform restaurants, bars, caterers etc about your allergies before ordering

Order simple dishes with few ingredients to avoid the risk of cross-contamination

Do not order fried food or stuffed pasta in restaurants

Avoid buffets

Be careful with cakes and desserts

Watch for cross-contamination in gelaterie

Learn the Italian words for risky foods

Note the 118 emergency number in case of a reaction

The Italian name of epinephrine is 'adrenalina'

KIDS' MEALS

For Italians, food and family are inseparable, so kids are welcome at any Italian restaurant. Italian children grow up at the dinner table: it is over food that they learn to listen and converse, develop an appreciation of good cuisine and learn the value of a shared meal.

Kids of all ages dine out in Italian restaurants, but this doesn't mean you'll find a child-friendly menu, high-chairs or changing tables in the bathroom. Italians expect families to dine together as they do at home, which might mean balancing babies on laps, adults sitting alongside children helping them when needed, and children participating in the same meal albeit in smaller quantities.

Even in fancy restaurants with formal wait staff, Italians are friendly and welcoming to families. While there may not be a children's menu, Italian food is generally uncomplicated, free of rich or complex sauces,

and bread, pasta and pizza are in bountiful supply. Very small children usually eat off their parents' plate, otherwise just ask for a *mezzo porzione* (half portion). Waiters may occasionally ask if you'd like a particular variation of pasta. If not, feel free to ask for simple options like *pasta al pomodoro* (pasta with tomato sauce) or pasta with oil and parmesan.

While Italy has no chain restaurants marketed as 'family friendly', there is always a neighbourhood pizzeria. Here you can be assured of piping hot, good quality, handmade dough that's topped, more often than not, with delicious organic ingredients and bubbling cheese. What's more, Italians expect children to participate fully in the experience of a meal, whether or not it goes on for hours. For long Sunday lunches, restaurants at agriturismos (farmhouses) are popular, as children can play outside between courses or at

BREASTFEEDING IN PUBLIC

In general, Italy isn't burdened with societal stigma with regard to breastfeeding. Feeding your baby is simply seen as a natural fact of life and few people, if any, will even notice. Furthermore, breastfeeding is depicted time and again in many of the country's most famous Renaissance artworks, such as Leonardo da Vinci's Madonna Litta. And, in recent years, Pope Francis himself has encouraged mothers to breastfeed in the Sistine Chapel during the collective January baptism that marks the baptism of Jesus. That said, in busy bars and cafés you may feel like being more discreet if you feel self-conscious.

Italian children GROW UP at the DINNER TABLE: it is over food that they learn TO LISTEN and converse

the end of the meal while the adults talk; in most cities you can find places with small gardens or close to nearby parks. Also, don't be surprised to see little kids still lingering while you finish off your after-dinner drink.

All in all, dining in an Italian restaurant as a family is a thoroughly enjoyable experience. Involving kids in meals not as 'special cases' but as budding diners and teaching them to value and enjoy good food and good company is a cultural priority in Italy. And you'll probably find that it is over the table of some friendly trattoria that your best memories are created.

From top: Children let off steam between courses; A plate of ravioli

FOREIGN FOOD

While Italian-style restaurants seem to have found a place in just about every other country in the world, Italians themselves seem quite content with what they've got. They are proud of their roots, and firmly believe that their Mediterranean diet is the best and most healthy of all.

While this seems rather inward looking on the surface, consider the diversity of regional Italian cuisine, which has been influenced by waves of immigrants over the centuries. Dishes in Sicily have clear Middle Eastern influences, for example, and the northern diet features Germanic, Austrian and French flavours. Tomatoes, chillies and chocolate were introduced to Italy from Latin America, and *baccalà* (salt cod) via the Baltic states, while dishes typical of towns on the eastern coast show some

Serbian, Albanian and Greek flair. As a result, Italians tend to think rather smugly that their food is the best in the world, which begs the question of why anyone would eat anything else. Furthermore, while Italy may have been unified in 1871, many Italians are still getting to know their own country's diverse regional recipes. For example, pizza was only introduced to Rome post-WWII by southern immigrants – so you're more likely to see a Sicilian, Piedmontese, Roman or Venetian restaurant in the capital than a French, Brazilian or Indian one.

Milan is Italy's most international city, and thanks to its increasingly diverse population, there is plenty of choice in terms of ethnic eateries. The restaurants run by Milan's historic Chinese community have now

moved beyond the cheap eats of Chinatown: gourmet places such as Dim Sum use prized Lombard ingredients, and dumpling shops like Ravioleria Sarpi draw queues that stretch around the block.

Vietnamese and Japanese restaurants are well represented in Milan as well. And Japanese sushi and ramen are increasingly popular in big cities, such as Rome and Florence, as they tap into the Italian love of *crudo* (raw fish or meat) and pasta in *brodo* (broth). Ethiopian food can also be found in Milan, Rome and Florence thanks to the presence of a longstanding Ethiopian community. And in all big cities you'll find Mexican, Lebanese, Indian and Greek restaurants.

More recent trends in foreign food include American-style brunch places, gourmet burger joints and steakhouses. And, in 2018, Starbucks opened their first Reserve Roastery in Milan, and now plans to expand across the country. However, outside of big cities, and in the south, locals prefer to stick to what they've tried and tested over the centuries.

STREET EATS

Italy isn't naturally associated with street food, which is strange considering not one, but two, of the most famous street foods in the world – pizza and ice-cream – are Italian. In fact, many of the most authentic Italian products – dried meats, salami, hard cheeses and all manner of dough products – were created as tasty treats to eat on the go.

As with the regular dining scene, Italian street food varies from region to region and reflects the environment, history and culture of each area. Once considered the food of peasants, labourers or factory workers, street food is newly fashionable and is available in many markets and food fairs up and down the country. Delis, bakeries and *rosticcerie* serve daily fresh sandwiches and fast-food snacks, while in cities like Milan, Rome and Florence, you'll find trendy food cart scenes. In central and southern Italy, mobile *rosticcerie* can be found in and around markets, and tripe carts are a historic fixture.

From top: Gelato is perfect strolling food; Browsing a Rome food market

NORTHERN ITALY

Leftover polenta, the northern Italian staple of cooked cornmeal, is a popular street food once sliced and fried. In Piedmont, try *goffre*, waffles stuffed with ham and cheese, or with honey, jam or chocolate; *farinata*, a chickpea pancake cooked in a wood-burning oven, is the pride of Genoa. In the Veneto, popular treats include fried *fritole* doughballs, seasoned with citrus zest, pine nuts and raisins; and fried, breaded *crema fritta* custard balls. In Venice, as in all Italian port cities, look out for paper cones of fish fried in a light flour batter.

CENTRAL ITALY

In the heart of Italy, Emilia-Romagna is famous for *piadina*, a flatbread traditionally cooked on a terracotta plate and stuffed with anything you like. *Lampredotto*, cow's stomach cooked in a broth of tomato, onion, celery and parsley and served on a Tuscan-style *smelle* bun, is the ultimate Florentine street food; and *castagnaccio*, chestnut-flour cake, is eaten all over Tuscany in autumn. Umbria and Le Marche are best known for their *olives all'ascolana* (breaded Ascolana olives stuffed with spiced meat), while Romans and Abbruzzese are suckers for *porchetta di Ariccia* (roasted pork) sandwiches and *supplì*, fried rice balls filled with tomato sauce, or ragù and melted mozzarella.

SOUTHERN ITALY

In Sicily, you'll find *panelle* (chickpea fritters) and *stigghiola*, a shishkebab-style skewer of lamb, goat or offal cooked on a wood-fired grill. There's also *pani ca meusa*, literally 'bread with spleen', topped with caciocavallo cheese and lemon juice (the Calabrian version, *panino con marzeddu*, is stuffed with veal offal and hot sauce). And then there's *arancini*, deep-fried stuffed rice balls similar to Roman *supplì*. In Puglia, there's *panzerotti*, a half-moon-shaped pastry filled with cheese and tomato, while Naples is the home of pizza, including *pizza a portafoglio* (folded pizza). *Sorbetteria*, mobile carts offering iced fresh lemon juice tempered with sugar, can be found all over, and *gelato con la brioche*, ice-cream in a brioche bun, is a real thing.

SPECIALITIES

One of the world's most famous cuisines, Italian food encompasses an enormous amount of regional variation, but remains utterly distinctive.

We can all instantly recognise a plate of Italian food: a light but fragrant seasoning of herbs and oil, and a striking simplicity.

Italy may be a country of a thousand bell towers – the common term *campanilismo* describes the Italian love of locality in the form of attachment to the local bell tower (*campanile*) – but the food of the peninsula has common roots in the Classical world of Greece and Rome, where local ingredients such as fish, game, herbs, fungi, olive oil, bread and wine were all prized.

The Greeks initiated the country's long wine tradition and planted Puglia's thousand-year-old olive trees, providing two heroes of the Italian table. The Romans were master bread bakers, excellent agriculturalists and experts in food preservation, introducing the use of brine and salt for pickling, oil and vinegar for preserving, and smoking and drying for the curing of meat and fish. Italy's panoply of charcuterie (here called salumi) and habit of preserving everything *sott'olio* (under oil) stems from the period, as do the Italian pastimes of foraging for wild greens, mushrooming and hunting for game birds.

Italy's dynamic cities also helped knit together common food habits, and from the Renaissance onwards urban kitchens were largely responsible for embracing radical new produce from overseas – from tomatoes, potatoes, peppers and citrus to wheat and rice. Chefs presiding over aristocratic kitchens were important people who helped to build the country's food identity and culture through recipe books (the first of these was published in Naples in the 13th century) that were widely distributed.

The most significant of these chefs was Pellegrino Artusi, whose *Science in the Kitchen and the Art of Eating Well* was published in Florence in the late 19th century, when the city was briefly the capital of the newly unified country. This classic of modern Italian cuisine is still a bestseller in Italy and has been translated into seven other languages. It shows tomatoes were enjoyed across Italy even then – as were potatoes, pasta and coffee.

Ironically, though, it wasn't until Italian migrants started leaving Italy in the great waves of emigration during the 19th century that the country's food identity was cemented. Although hybridized beyond recognition, America's love of and adoption of iconic Italian foods such as pizza, pasta, lasagne, meatballs, minestrone, osso buco, saltimbocca, parmesan, fettuccine al Fredo and ice-cream rocketed Italian food to global celebrity status. Finally, with the perspective of distance, much-loved local specialities could finally be seen as uniquely and distinctly Italian.

PASTA

Pasta arrived in Italy with the Arabs in the 9th century, but centuries of Italian invention, agriculture, industry, poverty and politics have shaped it into the myriad forms and flavours of today. There are now over 300 different pasta shapes, but subtle differences exist not only from region to region, but family to family.

Most pasta can be divided into two groups: *pasta fresca* (fresh pasta) and *pasta secca* (dry pasta). *Secca* is more typical of the traditionally poorer south, as it's made simply from semolina (durum wheat) flour and water. In the far south of the country, this basic dough is formed into chunky shapes by hand, while in Naples and south-central Italy, it's extruded by machine into long strands, sheets or complex shapes.

In the wealthier north and north-central Italy, expensive egg yolks and refined flours (usually *doppio*) are used to make silky ribbons and tiny, intricate stuffed shapes. Further north still, in mountainous regions under the influence of Germany, Austria and Eastern Europe, white flour is often replaced by other starches, such as chestnut, buckwheat or rye: the Valtellina's *pizzoccheri* noodles are made with buckwheat flour, for example.

The properties of each dough and the size and shape of individual pastas is also no accident. Each type of pasta absorbs sauce differently, and each shape is designed as part of a dish: you won't see Italians putting a *ragù* (meat sauce) with a pasta intended for seafood or vegetables. Fresh egg pasta is

SUNNY DAYS

Some of Italy's best artisanal pasta comes from the small town of Gragnano, around 30km (19 miles) southeast of Naples. A pasta-producing hub since the 17th century, Gragnano's main street was specifically built along the sun's axis so that the pasta put out to dry by the local pastifici (pasta factories) would reap a full day's sunshine.

GLUTEN GRAINS

Following WWII, Italy's ancient grano duro (hard wheat grains) were largely abandoned in favour of faster-growing, high-yield wheat cultivars that were easier to mass-produce. Unfortunately, the gluten in these modified grains is less digestible and has contributed to the rise in intolerance and coeliac disease. In contrast, the gluten in ancient wheats used in artisanal pasta has evolved with us over millennia, and does not cause the same problems.

usually eaten with slow-braised meats or rich sauces made with butter and/ or cheese; it's also used in lasagne and *minestra* soups. By contrast, dry pasta, which has more 'bite' due to the higher protein content of semolina flour, is usually served with runnier, vegetable-based sauces.

Good pasta must not be overcooked – the centre should remain slightly hard. Pasta cooked this way is called *al dente* ('on the tooth'), as it offers a little resistance when you bite into it rather than feeling mushy. Any self-respecting Italian will reject pasta that's not *al dente*. In addition, pasta shouldn't be under-tossed or over-sauced, nor should it be too wet or too dry. And all well-made pasta should have had time to absorb the sauce.

PASTA FRESCA

Right: Making tagliatelle in Bologna

The most popular types of pasta fresca are as follows:

BIGOLI

A thick version of spaghetti from the Veneto, made with wholemeal flour and usually served with an anchovy or meat sauce.

CANNELLONI

Pasta sheets rolled around a filling of minced meat or cheese and spinach, covered in béchamel sauce and baked.

GNOCCHI

Virtually every food culture has produced some kind of dumpling similar to Italian gnocchi, which can be made with flour or potato, and are typically served with tomato or meat-based sauces.

LASAGNE

One of the oldest types of pasta originating from the Roman dough *laganum*, it's now used as layers between meat, vegetable or cheese fillings in the classic baked dish.

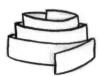

PAPPARDELLE

A wide, flat noodle from Tuscany. Often eaten during the winter hunting season and served with game-meat sauces of venison, boar and hare.

RAVIOLI

Originally from Liguria, ravioli are two square sheets of pasta sandwiched around a meat, cheese or vegetable filling. Raviolini are a smaller version, and ravioloni a larger one.

TAGLIATELLE

The most ubiquitous fresh pasta shape, these flat noodles can be cut to varying thicknesses. Similar versions include taglierini, tajarin and taglioni.

TORTELLINI

Originally from Bologna, these tiny meat-filled pasta packets are supposedly fashioned in the shape of Venus' belly button. Larger versions are usually stuffed with vegetarian fillings such as pumpkin and cheese.

PASTA SECCA

From top: Dry pasta comes in all shapes and sizes; A local cuisine shop in Gallipoli

The most popular types of pasta secca are as follows:

BUCATINI

Popular in Lazio and Calabria, this is a long, thin pasta similar to spaghetti, but has a hole down the centre. The name comes from the Italian word *bucato*, meaning 'with a hole'.

CAVATELLI

Originally found in Puglia (and, some say, Molise), these round, flat pasta discs are made by squashing small balls of dough with the heel of the hand. Usually served with a vegetable sauce.

LINGUINE

This long, thin pasta is similar to fettuccine, but slightly elliptical rather than flat, and is usually served with seafood or pesto. The name means 'little tongues'.

MACCHERONI

Macaroni pasta comes under this umbrella. It is often grooved to better retain the meat and cheese sauces that it's served with.

ORECCHIETTE

A Puglian pasta has curled edges and a domed centre that have earned it the name 'little ears'. It's typically served with wild turnip tops and broccoli, or a tomato sauce.

PENNE

A traditionally Roman pasta that takes its name from *penna* (pen), because the tip of the pasta looks like the nib of a fountain pen. It is best served with pesto and tomato-based sauces.

PICI

This thick, hand-rolled pasta, much like spaghetti, originates in Tuscany and is served with both vegetable and meat sauces. It is also referred to as pinci.

SPAGHETTI

Italy's most famous pasta is thought to have been introduced to Sicily by the Arabs. It is highly versatile and is served with seafood, tomato-based sauces and carbonara (egg, parmesan and pancetta).

BREADS, GRAINS & PULSES

BREADS

Bread (*pane*) is served at every meal but breakfast: you'll be given a basket of it in restaurants, and freshly cut chunks in Italian homes. It's used to moderate the richness of meals, and, most of the time, it will be white. Today, there are more than 250 different types of traditional Italian bread.

Usually, you'll find the bread is crusty, light and airy inside. Lovers of wholemeal should look for *pane integrale*, the general term for bread made with at least some proportion of wholemeal flour. On restaurant tables, you'll also see *grissini*, thin sticks of crispy bread made from a yeast-risen dough. While *grissini* usually come in packets, the really good ones are *fatto a mano* (made by hand) and served in bread baskets.

In the north, where wheat flour is common, you'll find soft, white bread. In Lombardy, rice flour may be used, and in Emilia-Romagna corn flour is more common. Liguria's oily focaccia is internationally acclaimed and is usually sprinkled with salt or herbs, while in northern Alto Adige, where there's a heavy German influence, *pane di segale* (rye bread) is common. And the typical unsalted bread of Tuscany is *pane sciocco*; a somewhat acquired taste, it's essential for the region's bread-thickened soups.

In the south, where durum wheat is preferred, the bread is chewier with a thick crust. The Puglian town of Altamura is famous for its naturally leavened bread made from re-milled durum wheat, which now has protected status. Roman poet Horace thought it the 'best bread in the world' back in 37 BCE.

MUSIC SHEETS

In Sardinia, look for the strangely named carta di musica *(music sheets), a crispy, paper-thin flatbread that has kept Sardinian shepherds fed for centuries. These crispy sheets are double-baked and feel like parchment, hence the name.*

GRAINS

Grains play a fundamental role in Italian cuisine. Even before there was wheat for flour there was *farro* (spelt), an ancient grain still in use today. One of the most popular grains is polenta, the cornmeal staple of the north, popularised after Christopher Columbus brought corn to Italy from the Americas during the late 1500s. Polenta is made by cooking cornmeal in stock or milk for up to an hour; the resulting paste can be enriched with butter or cheese, and served soft or hard.

The other great grain in Italy is, of course, rice. Food historians generally agree that rice came to Europe by way of India, and during the Roman era, it was an expensive commodity used in small quantities for medicinal purposes. The earliest documentation of rice growing in Italy dates to 1475, when its cultivation on the Lombard plain was promoted by Galeazzo Maria Sforza, Duke of Milan. Today, some 50 varieties of rice are grown in the Po Valley, and with a country-wide output of 1.33 million tonnes, Italy is Europe's largest rice producer. Among the best known varieties are *carnaroli*, a medium-grain rice mostly grown in Piedmont. Others, such as *arborio* (a short grain) and *vialone nano* (a thicker grain), are grown around Pavia.

Above: A paddy field in the grounds of Trauttmansdorff Castle in South Tyrol

PULSES

Dried beans are a staple across the country, but nowhere more so than in Tuscany, where they appear in traditional dishes like *minestra di fagioli* (bean soup), *minestra di pane* (bread and bean soup) and *ribollita* (reboiled bean, vegetable and bread soup with black cabbage). Packed with protein, cheap and available year-round (eaten fresh in summer, dried in winter), they were the poor man's 'meat' of choice.

Lentils (*lenticchie*) are the oldest of all Mediterranean pulses, their origins dating back more than 7000 years. They were immensely popular during the Roman era, so much so that the powerful Lentuli family derived their name from this humble pulse. Typically, lentils are cooked in soups, combined with rice or simply braised. The best variety is from the tiny Umbrian town of Castelluccio, although lentils are also grown in Molise and Abruzzo.

Of the dozens of other bean varieties, cannellini from Tuscany and borlotti from Veneto are the most popular. Borlotti beans are usually used in soups, while cannellini are perfect in salads or a stew. The round, yellow zolfino from Pratomagno and the silky-

ANCIENT GRAINS

Often translated as spelt, but also as emmer, farro is an ancient grain known to have been eaten by the Etruscans and many of the imperial Roman legions. It is a hard grain, higher in magnesium and protein than softer, more easily ground grains like wheat.

smooth sorano bean from Pescia are more highly prized, and the *fagioli dall'occhio* (black-eyed bean), cultivated in Europe since Etruscan times, is a rare treat.

Chickpeas (*ceci*) are also a historic staple, enjoyed by the Romans and still popular all over Italy, although the best recipes come from the south. There are a number of chickpea dishes, usually containing tomatoes and garlic and always dressed with olive oil; a salad of chickpeas and rocket is popular in Puglia, and in Rome chickpeas are sautéed in garlic-flavoured oil with rosemary and anchovies.

PIZZA

Much of Italy's no-nonsense attitude to food – keep it simple, keep it local and keep it coming – remains deeply rooted in the traditions of the poor. This is especially true in the country's predilection for pizza, a mainstay of *cucina povera* (poor man's cooking) and one of the foundations on which Italy's gastronomic reputation stands.

A derivation of the flatbreads of ancient Greece and Turkey, pizza was already a common street snack in Naples when the city's 16th-century Spanish occupiers introduced the tomato to Italy. The New World topping cemented pizza's popularity, and in 1738 Naples' first pizzeria opened its doors on Port'Alba, where it still stands. Soon after, the city's *pizzaioli* (pizza makers) began to enjoy minor celebrity status.

To this day, the city's most famous dough-kneader remains Raffaele Esposito, inventor of the classic Margherita pizza. As the city's top *pizzaiolo*, Esposito was summoned to fire up a treat for a peckish King Umberto I and his wife, Queen Margherita, on a royal visit in 1889. Determined to impress the Italian royals, Esposito based his creation of tomato, mozzarella and basil on the red, white and green flag of the newly unified Italy. The resulting topping met with the queen's approval and was subsequently named in her honour.

More than a century later, pizza purists claim that you really can't top Esposito's classic combo when it's made by a true Neapolitan *pizzaiolo*. Not everyone is in accordance, and Italians are often split between those who favour the thin-crust Roman variant and those who go for the thicker Neapolitan version.

Other more modern variations include *pizza al taglio* (pizza by the slice), popularised in Rome but now eaten throughout the country. Alternatively, there's the portable calzone, made using the same dough as a pizza, but folded in half around its fillings, most typically including salami or ham, mozzarella, ricotta and/or parmesan.

© Sezer Alcinkaya / Getty Images

64

PIZZA DOUGH

According to the official Associazione Verace Pizza Napoletana (True Neapolitan Pizza Association), genuine Neapolitan pizza dough must be made using highly refined type 00 wheat flour (a small dash of type 0 flour is permitted), compressed or natural yeast, salt, and water with a pH level between six and seven. While a low-speed mixer can be used for kneading the dough, only hands can be used to form the disco di pasta (pizza base), which should not be thicker than 3mm. The pizza itself should be cooked at 485°C (905°F) in a double-domed, wood-fired oven using oak, ash, beech or maple logs.

From top: A woman with an olive plant; Olive groves in Trentino

© Susan Wright / Lonely Planet

OLIVE OIL

Olive trees have been grown in the Mediterranean basin since the 8th century BCE, and olive oil has been a valuable commodity – used in everything from cosmetics and food to fuel and pharmaceuticals – since the days of the Roman Empire. Along with grapes and wheat, olive oil is one of three core Italian food products, and the country is now the world's second-largest producer.

Unlike many other countries, olive groves in Italy tend to be on small, independent farms with low-density planting. What's more, many trees are planted in geographically challenging places, so harvesting is arduous and quantities small, accounting for the high prices. This does, however, mean that Italy retains a great deal of biodiversity in its cultivars: around 350 varieties are grown here, and each is characterised by its own specific flavour.

OLIVE OIL 101

The best oils are made from hand-picked olives, which are often ground with stone mills and gently pressed between cotton mats. The best olive oil is *olio d'oliva extra-vergine* (extra-virgin olive oil). The classification for this is principally a chemical analysis, where the oleic acid content must be less than 1% – lower acid usually means more flavour and aroma. To be called extra-virgin, the oil is also required to be mechanically (as opposed to chemically) extracted.

The quality of olive oil depends on the region in which the olives are grown, their variety, their ripeness when picked, and the speed and method by which they are crushed. Filtration can clear a cloudy oil, but often removes the mouth-feel of a wonderful oil. The most sought-after oil is often that which runs free when olive paste is spread on stacked mats, before any pressure is applied. This free-run oil is usually more viscous, pungent and finer-tasting than the oil that comes later.

Olives harvested earlier in the season produce a greener oil, as there's more chlorophyll in the fresher fruit; those harvested later will produce a more golden oil. Likewise, green olives deliver bitter, fruitier oils, while riper olives tend to yield sweeter, milder oils.

FLAVOUR PROFILES

In general, there are three main flavour profiles:

DELICATE OIL

Made from Arbequina, Leccino, Sevillano and Taggiasca olives, and best suited to drizzling on fish.

MEDIUM INTENSITY OIL

Made from Ascolana, Manzanilla and Mission olives, and used for dressing salads, grilled vegetables, soups, sauces and poultry.

ROBUST OIL

Made from Arbosana, Frantoio and Picholine olives and used (with a squeeze of lemon) on red meat such as steak.

BUYING GUIDE

To some extent, the 'best' olive oils will depend on your own taste preferences. Single-estate oils from Tuscany are among the finest, and their taste reflects the care that goes into their production. Exceptional oil is not the sole preserve of the Tuscans, though. Great oils can also be found around Lake Garda, in Liguria, near Spoleto in Umbria, around Andria in Puglia and in Sicily. Olive oils are pressed in late autumn and early winter (November to December), and this is the best time to buy them. Use your oil up quickly – some say within two months of opening – as it doesn't age well. In fact, exposure to light hastens oxidisation and increases acidity, which is why most olive oils are sold in dark-green bottles.

THE BEST DOP and IGP Quality-Assured OLIVE OILS

GARDA DOP

Enormous Lake Garda, which crosses the borders of the Veneto, Lombardy and Trentino, has a wonderfully benign microclimate that's perfect for the Casaliva cultivar. This olive yields an oil that tastes of freshly-cut grass and almonds, with a distinct bitter finish.

RIVIERA LIGURE DOP

Made from the local Taggiasca olive, this is considered one of the best extra-virgin oils in the country. Olives here grow on steep terraces facing the sea and yield a delicate oil that is almost sweet to taste.

TOSCANO IGP

The only Italian olive oils given IGP status, those from Tuscany are among the country's best and are derived mainly from the Leccino and Frantoio varieties. The former gives an oil that is delicate, light and fruity, the latter an intensely herbaceous and pungent oil.

UMBRIA DOP

This classification covers the whole of Umbria and a number of varieties. The most important are San Felice, which yields a grassy oil with an artichoke flavour; and Moraiolo, which gives a fierce, bitter and almost spicy oil.

COLLINE PONTINE DOP

Grown south of Rome on hills overlooking the sea, the Itrana olive is a recent addition to the DOP list, and produces an oil with herbal overtones and a distinct taste of semi-ripe tomatoes.

COLLINE DELL'UFITA DOP

Originating in Campania, where olive trees grow pretty much everywhere, this oil comes from the Ravece olive. The flavour is intense and well-balanced, with scent of ripe tomatoes, making it perfect for drizzling on pizza.

TERRA DI BARI DOP

Southern Puglia is covered in olive trees, which yield some 30% of Italy's total olive crop. Some of the best, based on the Coratina variety, are grown around Bari and produce an oil with a strong and punchy character.

LAMETIA DOP

Similar to Puglia, Calabria is a major olive producing region. The premium Carolea cultivar is grown around Lamezia Terme, and yields a surprisingly gentle, fruity oil with hints of green apples and almonds.

MONTI IBLEI DOP

With its rich volcanic soils, Sicily has an abundance of excellent olive oils. The best comes from the Tonda Ilbea olives grown near Mount Etna, which produce oils with a fruity, ripe-tomato aroma.

SARDEGNA DOP

Covering almost the whole island of Sardinia, this DOP accreditation covers four olive varieties. The best of these is the Bosana, a robust, temperature-resistant tree that gives polyphenol-rich oils with a bitter taste that is balanced against notes of artichoke.

ITALIAN OLIVE OIL: THE NUMBERS

→ Italy produces around 400,000 tonnes of olive oil each year

→ Only 40% of Italian extra-virgin olive oil is exported

→ In the 18 Italian regions where olive trees grow, there are roughly 902,000 farms, 179 million olive trees and 4500 pressing mills

→ Italy produces 42 DOP-protected oils and one IGP-protected oil

BALSAMIC

Originally used by the Romans to preserve food, balsamic vinegar (*aceto balsamico*) was virtually unheard of outside central Italy until the 20th century.

Today, true balsamic is only made in the towns of Reggio Emilia and Modena, and is protected by the EU's DOP status. Contrary to what the name might suggest, there is no balsam in balsamic vinegar. The name simply means 'balsam-like' in the sense of something restorative, as this sweet vinegar, made from cooked grape 'must' (grapes pressed with their skins and stems), was initially sipped after dinner as a health cordial or *digestivo*. Two consortiums, one in Modena and one in Reggio Emilia, protect and regulate the production of balsamic vinegar, which involves the extraction and boiling down of just-harvested Trebbiano (and, sometimes, Lambrusco) grape must into a thick syrup called *mosto cotto* (cooked must), with a minimum sugar concentration of 30%. The must is then fermented over years in a series of barrels decreasing in size and made from a variety of wood: cherry, mulberry, chestnut, oak, ash and juniper.

The barrels are stored in attic spaces which can reach 50°C (122°F) in summer, causing the must to evaporate and condense and the flavour to intensify, with the vinegar becoming extremely sweet and viscous as it matures. After a minimum of 12 years, a small portion is drawn off the smallest cask, which is then topped-up (as are all the casks) with some vinegar from the next largest barrel. This process is repeated every year.

The resulting balsamic is a rich, glossy, deep-brown colour and has a complex flavour that balances the natural sweet and sour elements of the *mosto cotto* with tannins from the various wooden casks. You'll find it typically aged for 12, 18 and 25 years, and bottles of true balsamic should carry the label 'Aceto Balsamico Tradizionale di Modena/Reggio Emilia'; the addition of 'Extra Vecchio' to the name denotes the 'Extra Old' 25-year-matured vintage.

Because only 10% of what is drawn off is deemed of suitable quality, the rest is usually watered down with red wine vinegar and sold as cheaper *condiment balsamico*, *salsa balsamico* or *salsa di mosto cotto*.

Balsamic vinegar is typically used sparingly, either dripped on strong cheese, like parmesan, or to enhance pastas, risottos, steak, eggs or fish. It might also be drizzled on strawberries or pears, or atop creamy desserts such as zabaglione, panna cotta and crème caramel.

PRODUCE
Winter

WHAT'S IN SEASON

Artichokes (*carciofi*), beans (*fagioli*), cabbage (*cavolo*), carrots (*carote*), onions (*cipolle*), cauliflower (*cavolfiore*), fennel (*finocchio*), kale (*cavolo riccio*), lentils (*lenticchie*), potatoes (*patate*), rapini/turnip greens (*broccoli rapa*), spinach (*spinaci*), clementines (*clementine*), mandarins (*mandarini*), oranges (*arancie*), pears (*pere*), persimmons (*cachi*), pomegranates (*melagrane*), almonds (*mandorle*).

DECEMBER

As the most flavourful cabbage is thought to be that harvested after a frost, December is cabbage season – look out for the famous *cassoeula* (pork and cabbage stew) in Lombardy or sauerkraut in cities and towns throughout the Dolomites. Another stunningly good winter vegetable, chicory (*radicchio*) adds a bitter, spicy note to salads and is also served grilled.

JANUARY

Sweet Sicilian oranges bring some sunshine to January mornings: order a fresh *spremuta d'arancia* (squeezed orange juice) at breakfast time. You'll also find an abundance of clementines and mandarins during this period, which are especially good in desserts and as gelato flavours.

FEBRUARY

Two more stars arrive at the market in February: beautiful bunches of broccoli and fennel – a staple of Italian cooking, flavouring bread, soups and salads, or simply cooked in olive oil and served as a side. The broccoli-like rapini, or turnip greens, takes pride of place in the Pugliese favourite *orecchiette con le cime di rapa*. Almonds are also harvested in the south this month, used to decorate pies and cakes.

From left: Artichokes are available in winter and spring, but peak in April; A Campania lemon producer

spring

WHAT'S IN SEASON

Artichokes (*carciofi*), asparagus (*asparagi*), beans (*fagioli*), beetroot (*barbabietole*), courgette/zucchini flowers (*fiori di zucca*), fava beans (*fave*), garlic (*aglio*), leeks (*porri*), spring peas (*piselli*), cherries (*ciliegie*), kiwi (*kiwi*), lemons (*limoni*), strawberries (*fragole*)

MARCH

This is the last month in which fresh pumpkin and radicchio are available, but root dishes are rapidly giving way to lighter greens. In the north, beetroots are already growing and even asparagus begins to make an appearance, though it won't hit peak flavour for a few more months. The star of March is the leek, cooked in dozens of different ways: leek and potato soup, flavoured with pancetta, is a highlight.

APRIL

April is the peak time for globe artichokes – a beloved Italian vegetable that takes menus and markets by storm this month. You can try artichokes in soups, savoury pies or risottos, but perhaps the best way to celebrate them is with *carciofi alla giudia*, the Jewish-Roman way: tenderized then deep-fried.

MAY

Though they begin sprouting in March, May is the best time to dive into asparagus – you can find both the green and the more coveted white asparagus on menus, and the flavour of both is at its peak. Asparagus, fava beans and pecorino served together are a Roman favourite, but in Milan they prefer *asparagi alla Milanese*, with a boiled egg. Cherries also hit markets for a fleeting moment between May and June.

summer

WHAT'S IN SEASON

Aubergine/eggplant (*melanzane*), basil (*basilico*), courgette/zucchini flowers (*fiori di zucca*), courgette/zucchini (*zucchine*), cucumbers (*cetrioli*), peas (*piselli*), peppers (*peperoni*), tomatoes (*pomodori*), apricots (*albicocca*), berries (*frutti di bosco*), cantaloupe melon (*melone*), figs (*fichi*), peaches (*pesche*), plums (*susini*), watermelon (*cocomero/anguria*) and lemons (*limoni*).

JUNE

Take advantage of the season's courgette (zucchini) production and eat the flowers! *Fiori di zucca* is a perfect appetizer when fried and stuffed with ricotta, but you can enjoy them roasted, in a risotto, on pizza or baked into focaccia. Sicily's strawberries (*fragole*) ripen in May, but further north they are at their best in June – prime time to indulge in strawberry gelato on a hot afternoon.

JULY

Continue to enjoy summer vegetables all through July – it's the fruits that change through the summer months. Wild blueberries (*mirtillo*) are harvested in July and begin to feature on menus, along with other forest berries, apricots and melons. Do as the Italians and survive the summer heat with a simple meal of fresh melon and prosciutto.

AUGUST

In August, tomatoes and aubergines (eggplant) reign supreme. Order the bruschetta, the caprese salad or a tomato tart to enjoy the most flavour from fresh tomatoes. Try *melanzane alla parmigiana* (layered aubergine and parmesan), or a classic Sicilian caponata: cooked aubergine sweetened with vinegar. Be on the lookout for lemons, too, particularly on the Amalfi Coast, where the world-famous crop is in season.

From left: Baked aubergine (eggplant); Roasting chestnuts; A successful truffle hunt

Autumn

WHAT'S IN SEASON

Chestnuts (*castagne*), fennel (*finocchio*), mushrooms (*funghi*), porcini mushrooms (*porcini*), pumpkin (*zucca*), spinach (*spinaci*), tenderstem broccoli (*broccoletti*), truffles (*tartufi*), apples (*mele*), figs (*fichi*), grapes (*uva*), prunes (*prugne*).

SEPTEMBER

This month's highlight is the porcini mushroom, used in stews, soups, pasta and pizza, or simply platters or sides of roasted porcini alone. Though porcini foragers have likely been out in the woods since July, September is the main month for mushrooms to hit restaurants. Figs get their second harvest in the south of Italy, which specialises in the sweet, green variety. September also marks the start of the grape harvest.

OCTOBER

In central and southern Italy, October temperatures remain warm, but in the north the first snows can arrive. Summer's slower-growing fruits and vegetables feature on Italian tables, and pumpkins are at their peak – find them in classic tortellini pasta or ravioli di zucca, especially in Emilia-Romagna or Lombardy. October is also the first month for the chestnut and its sweeter cousin, *marrone* – one of Italy's most beloved street foods.

NOVEMBER

The bounty of the summer might be missed, but November has its own treat: truffle season in northern Italy. Though October marks the start of the season, the *Tartufo Bianco d'Alba* – the country's most famous white truffle – is celebrated in Alba with a *sagra* (food festival) that runs until the end of November. Enjoy the earthy flavour of truffles shaved over pasta or an omelette, or stirred into a thick sauce for steak.

FUNGHI

In autumn, cars parked by woods or in obscure rural locations are usually a sign that the time is right for going mushroom picking (*andare a funghi*). While Italians may sometimes share their traditional mushroom recipes, they'll never reveal their favourite foraging spots.

There are several hundred types of fungi growing in the hills of Italy, most typically in the country's mountainous north and centre – fungi need cool weather and moisture to thrive. Over 50 species are edible, including the black and white *tartufi* (truffle), the true porcini (*boletus edulis*) and its related species, galletti (*cantharellus cibarius*) and cardoncelli (*pleurotus eryngii*), as well as wood blewits (*tricholoma nudum*) and other brightly coloured varieties.

The chestnut, pine, oak and beech forests of the Alps and Apennines offer the ideal habitat for fungi. Each forager is allowed to pick 3kg (6.6lb) of mushrooms a day, and many claim to find over 100kg (220.5lb) of mushrooms in a season, preserving their collection by drying or placing them *sott'olio*

(under oil) for the year ahead. Be aware, though, that several Italians die every year from eating toxic mushrooms – don't pick or even touch any species that you are unsure of.

The most popular mushroom is the porcini, which grows in abundance in the Apennines from the beginning of summer and into autumn. Fleshy and woodsy, it can be eaten raw in salads, grilled on meats, fried and sautéed with garlic; it's also often dried and is one of the main ingredients of risotto.

In the south, cardoncelli mushrooms are equally popular. Given their meaty character, they are often roasted or fried and added to pasta sauces. Galletti (chanterelle) are more flavourful and are often used to add depth to dishes; they are also a rich source of vitamin D.

TOP TRUFFLE EXPERIENCES

Barbialla Nuova, Montaione
This biodynamic farmstay is Tuscany's golden ticket for hunting white truffles.

Boutique del Tartufo, Volterra
Truffle shop selling fresh and conserved truffles, made-to-order truffle-infused cheese panini, truffle paste and so forth.

Pepenero, San Miniato
Celebrity chef Gilberto Rossi gives truffles a creative spin in his much-lauded restaurant.

Consorzio Turistico Langhe Monferrato Roero
Alba-based consortium that can hook you up with trifulau for an afternoon of truffle-hunting.

TARTUFI

They're not a plant, they don't spawn like mushrooms and cultivating them is virtually impossible. Pig-ugly yet precious, *tartufi* (truffles) are said to have aphrodisiacal qualities, and one whiff of their aroma is enough to convince one of their seductive qualities. They typically grow in the forests of northern Piedmont and in central areas of Tuscany, Le Marche and Umbria.

Truffles grow in symbiosis with oak, willow, hazelnut and poplar trees and come in two varieties: *bianco* (white – actually a mouldy old yellowish colour) or *nero* (black – a gorgeous velvety tone). Black truffles are less expensive and have two seasons, November to March and May through to September, while white truffles are in season primarily between October and January. The taste varies too, with white truffles having a strong earthy, nutty, honey flavour, while black truffles are often said to taste like earthy chocolate. Typically, truffles are served raw or thinly shaved over simple, mild-tasting dishes such as pasta, eggs or risotto.

Italy is one of the world's largest producers and exporters of truffles. Truffle hunting is an ancient tradition here and hunters (*trifulau*) use specially trained dogs to sniff out the tubers. Once found they are whisked to market quickly, as they are perishable. The country's most famous truffle fair is the International Alba White Truffle Fair in Piedmont, which is held on weekends throughout October and November.

Typically **TRUFFLES** are served raw OR THINLY SHAVED over simple, **MILD-TASTING DISHES**

77

SALUMI

Salumi (cured meat) is a broad term that takes in all Italian cold cuts, predominantly made with pork but also including cured-beef *bresaola* along with *salsiccia* (sausages) and cooked products such as mortadella.

Salumi is often described simply as *nostrano*, meaning 'ours' or 'local', and many families still make their own. There are dozens of different types of salumi, but the list below includes some of the most common.

BRESAOLA

Air-dried loin of raw beef cured with salt, black pepper and herbs; it can also be made from horse meat (*equino*).

CAPOCOLLO

Made using the neck muscle of the pig and salted for four to eight days. Can be spiced with red wine, pepper and herbs.

COPPA

A cut of pork neck spiced with cloves, laurel seeds, cinnamon and pepper, and left to season for six months.

CULATELLO

The finest cut of pork from beneath the buttocks, cured with salt, garlic and pepper and air-cured over 10 months.

LARDO

Quite simply, pork lard that has be aromatised with spices and seasoned in marble tubs for six to 10 months. The varieties from Arnaud in Valle d'Aosta and tiny Colonnata are most famous.

MORTADELLA

A very large sausage made with finely ground pork from the finest cuts of ham, and studded with lard and black pepper. It's sold in thin slices.

NDUJA

A very spicy, soft, spreadable salami paste made from pork, fat and lots of chilli peppers. It comes from Calabria and is a vibrant red colour. Use sparingly.

PANCETTA

Cured belly pork, similar to unsmoked bacon, which is usually coated in a rub typical of the region. In Calabria, this might be chilli; in Umbria they simply use a black pepper rub.

PROSCIUTTO COTTO

Cooked ham that is similar to English-style baked or boiled hams. Bright pink, it has a lighter flavour than prosciutto *crudo*. The northern Italian versions are best.

PROSCIUTTO CRUDO

Preserved ham from the hind leg of a female pig, prosciutto is still cured in mountain air for one year beneath a coating of flour, lard, salt and pepper.

SOPPRESSATA

Soppressata means 'pressed', and this leg- and shoulder-meat sausage, similar to salami but usually seasoned with chilli, is compacted once prepared.

SPECK

A dry-cured ham, gently smoked over several months using low-resin wood to ensure the meat stays sweet. It is typical of the Alto Adige.

MEAT & SEAFOOD

MEAT

Although Italians are not in the habit of eating as much meat (*carne*) as their fellow Europeans, meat (and seafood) are still the preeminent and most highly prized part of a meal, and the element against which the significance of all other foods is defined.

From the Middle Ages onwards, pork (*suino*) was the principle meat at all levels of Italian society, and forests were measured largely in terms of how many pigs they could sustain. Sheep, by contrast, were kept in order to provide milk and wool, although a milk-fed lamb (*abbacchio*) was often served at Easter. Game, meanwhile – including venison, wild boar, hare and dozens of wildfowl – was originally considered an aristocratic delicacy.

Thanks to the country's numerous rivers, lakes and lagoons, all manner of birds are eaten, including pigeon (*piccione*), partridges (*fagiano*), quail (*quaglia*), duck (*anatra*), guinea fowl (*faraona*) and turkey (*tacchino*). Goose (*oca*) has been a popular eating bird since Roman times and remains a common dish in the northern provinces of Friuli, Veneto, Lombardy and Emilia-Romagna. The famous *Salame d'Oca* from Mortara is now protected as a Slow Food product.

Beef (*manzo*) only started to feature on Italian menus toward the end of Middle Ages, as cities grew, forests diminished and grazing land became available. Italy's most famous beef dish is the epic Florentine T-bone steak, *bistecca alla Fiorentina*. Veal (*vitello*) is another popular speciality, as it's considered a healthier option. In the south and in the Alps, goat and the goat-like chamois are also eaten.

Clockwise from left: *Bistecca alla Fiorentina*; Lake Como; Grilled squid with asparagus and potatoes; Sea urchins caught off Bari

SEAFOOD

With 7600km (4722 miles) of coastline and dozens of large freshwater lakes and rivers, it is inevitable that fish (*pesce*) should feature heavily on Italian menus. However, the consumption of fish here is also inextricably linked to the liturgical calendar, which dictated that on certain 'lean' (*magro*) days, the faithful should forsake meat products. As a result, fish soon became the symbol of the monastic diet, and was considered not just healthy but downright virtuous.

Ancient fish tanks at the market near the Forum attest to the Roman love of fish, although at the time, given that commerce was largely confined to the Mediterranean, mainly saltwater fish was consumed. This changed during the Middle Ages, when freshwater varieties such as trout (*trota*), tench (*tinca*), perch (*persico*) and eel (*anguilla*) rose to prominence in recipe books.

These days, it is locally sourced, zero-kilometre fish that holds the most elevated gastronomic status thanks to its nutritional value and perishability. As you travel around, look out for regional specialities such as Liguria's red prawns (*gambero rosso*), Venice's razor clams (*vongole di rasio*) and mantis shrimps (*gambero di mantide*) or Puglia's sea urchins (*ricci di mare*) and mussels (*cozze*), as well as eels from the Valli di Comacchio, lavarello and perch around Lake Como, cuttlefish (*seppie*) in Liguria, Tuscany and Venice, tuna (*tonno*) and swordfish (*pescespada*) in Sicily, and Sardinia's red mullet (*triglia rossa*) and octopus (*polipo*).

81

CHEESE

Historically, Italians viewed cheese (*formaggio*) as a food of the poor, largely because it was eaten by peasants and shepherds as a substitute for meat. But because cheese was also regarded, ironically, as a 'lean' food by the church and permitted during Lent and on days of abstinence, it gained an important and elevated role in the Italian diet. Over time, and given the country's natural gastronomic curiosity and creativity, cheese production evolved into today's astonishing array of flavours and textures.

Northern Italian Cheese

ASIAGO

Hailing from Vicenza, Trento, Padua and Treviso, the pungent, full-flavoured Asiago DOP uses unpasteurised cow's milk from the Asiago plateau. Choose between milder, fresh *pressato* and strong, crumbly, aged *d'allevo*. The latter can be enjoyed at various stages of maturation, from sweeter *mezzano* (aged four to six months) and more bitter *vecchio* (aged over 10 months) to spicy *stravecchio* (aged for over two years).

BAGÒSS

Produced in Brescia from Bruna cows' milk, this is a well-matured, straw-coloured cheese traditionally prepared in herders' huts in the summer mountain pastures. It has a grassy aroma and an almond taste with a slightly spicy finish, and is protected as a Slow Food Presidia product (a category that aims to preserve traditional methods).

BITTO

An ancient Alpine cheese from the Valtellina Valley, made from a mixture of cow's milk and milk from the local Orobic goat, a breed now at risk of extinction. The mix is poured into copper moulds and aged to produce a dry, sharp flavour.

FONTINA

Made in the Aosta Valley since the 12th century, this mild, nutty cheese has fresh, grassy notes and a hint of honey. It features in nearly every local dish – including fondue, when it's mixed with eggs and milk into which you dip toasted bread.

GORGONZOLA

Gloriously pungent, this washed-rind, blue-veined cheese has been produced in Lombardy and Piedmont since the Middle Ages. Made using whole cow's milk, it's generally aged three to four months. Varieties include the younger, sweeter gorgonzola *dolce* and the sharper, spicier *piccante* (also known as *stagionato* or *montagna*).

MASCARPONE

A versatile triple-cream cheese made in Lodi and used to make desserts – including Italy's famed tiramisu.

MONTASIO

A semi-aged Alpine cheese made in northeast Italy with unpasteurised cow's milk. It has a mild, fruity, nutty flavour and it is the key ingredient in the region's *Friulano frico* (cheese and potato pie).

PROVOLONE

Though its roots lie in the southern Basilicata region, this semi-hard, wax-rind staple is now commonly produced in Lombardy and the Veneto. Like mozzarella, it's made using the *pasta filata* method, which sees the curd heated until it becomes stringy (*filata*). Aged for two to three months, provolone *dolce* is milder and sweeter than the piquant *piccante*.

STRACCHINO

One of Lombardy's most widely eaten cheeses, the name is derived from *stracca*, meaning tiredness – it's said that the milk of tired cows (during the seasonal move to and from Alpine pastures) is richer in fats and acids, giving stracchino its tang. It's usually eaten as a dessert cheese.

TALEGGIO

A semi-soft cheese originally made in the Talleggio Valley north of Bergamo. Soft and pungent, it's matured for six to 10 weeks to create a pinkish-grey rind. It has a mild, tangy taste and fruity finish.

Central Italian cheeses

CAPRINO
A broad term for all cheeses made from un-pasteurised goat's milk, which come either *fresco* (fresh) or *stagionato* (ripened). Some *caprini* are buttery and yellow with hints of lemon, while firmer varieties are more tangy and goaty.

FORMAGGIO DI FOSSA
A classic mixed-milk cheese from Emilia-Romagna, fossa is made from equal parts sheep and cow's milk, and is aged for three months in dark, straw-lined pits dug into volcanic *tufo* rock. The cheeses are traditionally retrieved at the end of November for the feast of Santa Caterina.

PARMIGIANO REGGIANO
Parmesan, Italy's most famous DOP-protected cheese, is produced in Parma, Reggio Emilia, Modena, Bologna and Mantua using milk from free-range (or grass/hay-fed) cows. It has a grainy texture and nutty flavour, and is available *fresco* (aged less than 18 months), *vecchio* (aged 18 to 24 months) and *stravecchio* (aged 24 to 36 months).

PECORINO
A sheep's milk cheese made near Rome for nearly 2000 years, pecorino is distinctive, strong and salty. Served with spicy or creamy pasta sauces, pecorino varieties range from sweet and caramel-like to tart and peppery.

RICOTTA
Literally meaning 're-cooked', this fresh cheese is lumpy and white in appearance, creamy on the palate and sweet to the taste. It's used in desserts such as *cannoli* and *pastiera*, as well as vegetarian pasta dishes.

Clockwise from left: Pecorino on sale; A cheese shop in Alba, Piedmont; Mozzarella

Southern Italian cheeses

CACIOCAVALLO

A semi-hard, stretched-curd (*pasta filata*) cheese produced all over the Italian south, caciocavallo is encased in a thin, hard crust and ranges from a sweet butterscotch taste to piquant and savoury. The most famous version is made with the milk of Podolico cows, aged for six to nine months, and has notes of cut grass, vanilla and spices.

FIORE SARDO

Made from the milk of the Sarda sheep, this hard, grainy cheese tastes of salty caramel. It's aged near a hot brazier for two weeks, after which the rind is washed with wine vinegar, olive oil and salt and stamped with the image of a flower – hence the name.

MOZZARELLA

A chewy, silky cheese, synonymous with Campania and Puglia and best eaten on the day it's made. Top of the range is luscious, porcelain-white DOP *mozzarella di bufala* (buffalo mozzarella), produced using the whole milk of black water buffaloes. Variations include *burrata*, buffalo-milk mozzarella filled with cream; *fior di latte* is mozzarella made using cow's milk.

RICOTTA SALATA

When ricotta ages it becomes hard and pungent, transforming it into the 'salted ricotta' that's used widely in southern Italy. In Sicily, it's grated over pastas such as the island's signature *pasta alla Norma*, which has an aubergine, tomato and basil sauce.

CHEESE LEXICON

Dolce *Sweet, signifying a young cheese with a honeyed, often nutty taste*

Pastorizzato *Pasteurised. Not all cheeses are – if this is a concern, ask the vendor*

Piccante *Piquant, meaning the cheese is sharp, often aged and sometimes acidic*

Stagionato *Aged*

Vecchio *Old*

Stravecchio *Really old*

SWEETS & GELATO

'Siamo arrivati alla frutta' ('we've arrived at the fruit') is an end-of-the-meal idiom roughly meaning 'we've hit rock bottom' – but hey, not until you've had one last tasty morsel.

After fresh, seasonal fruit, your best bets on the sweet (*dolci*) menu are creamy puddings like tiramisu or panna cotta, fruit-filled tarts (*crostate*) and cakes (*torte*), or standout pastries such as *cannoli*. The other popular options are, of course, seasonal gelato or some simple twice-baked biscotti to nibble on with your coffee or dip in your dessert wine.

Given the quality of the country's pastry shops, many Italians simply buy dessert from the nearest *pasticceria*, although *crostate* are usually homemade.

BABÀ

This airy, syrup-soaked sponge cake with its mushroom shape is a Neapolitan favourite, considered a symbol of Naples' culinary heritage despite its Polish origins.

CANNOLI

An ancient Carnival recipe originating in Sicily, these deep-fried, tube-shaped shells (originally shaped using river cane, hence the name) are filled with a creamy mix of ricotta and sugar. Different areas may further enhance them with chocolate chips, candied fruit, chopped almonds or pistachios.

CASSATA

The king of Sicilian desserts, cassata is a domed cake filled with sweetened ricotta that is flecked with candied fruits, vanilla and pistachio, and encased within a marzipan dome.

CROSTATA RICOTTA E VISCIOLE

Although fruit- and jam-filled shortcrust pastry tarts (*crostata*) can be found up and down the peninsula, *crostata ricotta* is a Roman Jewish tradition.

PANNA COTTA

Originating in Piedmont, this is one of the simplest Italian desserts, literally 'cooked cream' that's flavoured with vanilla and topped with fruit. It is thickened with gelatine, which gives its wobbly appearance.

PASTICCIOTTO LECCESE

Not dissimilar to the Portuguese *pastéis de Nata* (custard tart), this mini pastry tart from the Puglian town of Lecce is filled with *crema pasticciera* (egg custard) and sometimes preserved sour cherries.

SBRISOLONA

This so-called 'crumbly' cake originates in the northern town of Mantua and is made with a mix of corn and wheat flour, chopped almonds and whopping amounts of butter, enriched with sugar, eggs and lemon zest. Break chunks off with your hand and pair with a glass of grappa.

ZABAIONE

In its most traditional form, *zabaione* (also known as zabaglione) is made from egg yolk, sugar and Marsala wine, though other dessert wines such as Moscato, Porto or Vin Santo can also be used. It's served in little glass cups and topped with berries, chocolate shavings or crumbled amaretto biscuits.

PANETTONE

Milan's famous Christmas cake is really a sweet bread made of a yeast-risen dough flavoured with vanilla, zested peel, candied lemon and fruit such as raisins. As it ages, it can be toasted, but it's usually served in wedges with sweet wine like Moscato.

SEADAS

Sardinia is an island of shepherds, so the favourite dessert here naturally combines cheese and honey. Fresh cow or ewe cheese is stuffed into a puff-pastry shell, which is then deep-fried and served hot drizzled with honey.

TIRAMISU

Italy's most famous dessert, this richly layered, coffee-soaked savoiardi (sponge finger) and mascarpone pudding is topped with dusted cocoa, and sometimes enhanced with a drop of liqueur or rum. It is served in a glass or cup and the consistency should be luxuriously smooth.

ZUPPA INGLESE

'English soup' is actually an Italian version of trifle, made with sponge cake dipped in Alchermes (a reddish herbal liqueur) that's layered with lemon-scented crema pasticciera (cream custard), and sometimes chocolate cream or fruit compote.

From top: The flavours of Naples; Enjoying *gelato* in Florence

HANDMADE GELATO iS SOLD
up and down
THE PENiNSULA
and still outsells
iNDUSTRIALLY PRODUCED
iCE—CREAM

GELATO

The origins of ice-cream probably lie in Middle Eastern *sarbat* (sherbet), a concoction of sweet fruit syrups chilled with iced water which the Arabs brought to Sicily when they occupied the island in the 9th century. In Sicily, they found an enormous natural freezer in the near year-round snows of Etna, which provided the ice for *granita* (crushed ice mixed with fruit juice, coffee or almond milk) and *cremolata* (fruit syrups chilled with iced milk). From there it was just a short step to *semifreddo* (literally 'semi-frozen'; a cold, creamy dessert) and then gelato.

These days, handmade gelato (*gelato artigianale*) is sold up and down the peninsula in gelaterie, and still outsells industrially produced ice-cream. Unlike ice-cream, gelato contains less cream and fewer (or no) eggs. It is also churned at a slower rate, making it less aerated and denser, and it is stored at around -5°C (23°F), meaning it isn't completely frozen. This gives it a softer, silkier texture. Since gelato has less fat and is served at a warmer temperature, the flavour (whether it be pistachio or chocolate) presents more intensely in the mouth.

SORBETS GALORE

By the 17th century, sorbet was already popular in Venice, Rome and Naples. In 1775, the first book of recipes, Filippo Baldini's De Sorbetti, was published in Naples, and included sorbets made with lemon, orange and strawberry, as well as chocolate, cinnamon, coffee and pistachio. There's even a chapter dealing with milky sorbets – meaning ice-creams.

Popular flavours

At many gelaterie (ice-cream shops), you'll need to pay at the cash register before you order. Ask for a cono (cone) or a coppa (cup) and suggest a size – piccolo (small), medio (medium) or grande (large) – or a number of flavours you want to try (un gusto, due gusti...one flavour, two flavours...). Here are some of the most popular options:

Albicocca *Apricot*

Arancia *Orange*

Bacio *Chocolate with hazelnut pieces*

Banana *Banana*

Caffè *Coffee*

Cioccolato *Chocolate*

Cocco *Coconut*

Crema *Milk, cream and egg yolks*

Fior di latte *Cream sweetened with sugar*

Fragole *Strawberry*

Frutti di bosco *Fruits of the forest: berries*

Gianduia *Smooth hazelnut chocolate*

Limone *Lemon*

Melone *Melon*

Nocciola *Hazelnut*

Panna *Cooked cream*

Pesca *Peach*

Pistacchio *Pistachio*

Stracciatella *Vanilla with chocolate swirled through it*

Zabaione *Marsala with egg yolk*

SPECIALITY SHOPS

Italy is still a country full of small stores specialising in particular products, from salumi or cheese to bread or wine. These sit alongside weekly markets and lend Italian towns their vivacious character.

On entering a shop, greet the staff with *'buon giorno'* ('good day') or *'buona sera'* ('good evening'). In larger shops you can then help yourself, but in smaller stores or delis you may need to tell the proprietor what you want and they will assist you.

In fruit and vegetable shops, only touch the produce that you intend to buy – point to the items you'd like. In supermarkets you'll need to weigh your fruit and veg before taking it to the checkout.

Italy uses the decimal system, so prices are usually by the *chilo* (kilo), or by the *etto* (100 grams). Most small shops close early one day a week, and most are open on Sundays. You can also expect them to close for a few hours in the middle of the day.

Types of specialist shops

ALIMENTARI

A good *alimentari* is like a boutique supermarket, selling oils, cheese and salumi as well as dry goods and basics such as water. Really good *alimentari* will have a deli counter full of pre-prepared *antipasti*, as well as table olives and pickled vegetables.

CARNE EQUINE

The horse butcher. Seen more typically in the south, and selling all kinds of cuts (names are similar to those used for beef).

CASEIFICIO

This is usually the place where cheese is made, but most producers have an on-site shop and sell direct to the public.

ENOTECA

Meaning 'place of wine', an *enoteca* is both a wine store and/or a bar serving glasses of wine; good ones will generally offer wine tastings. Wine can also be bought at *alimentari* and supermarkets.

FORMAGGERIA/ LATTERIA

Shops selling milk and milk products such as cheese, cream and butter. They will always have parmesan, mozzarella, ricotta and a selection of local cheeses – and they should give you a taste (*assaggio*) before you buy.

FRUTTA E VERDURA

Fruit and vegetable shops. These tend to be found tucked into small streets and are often within striking distance of a *macelleria*, making shopping relatively easy.

MACELLERIA

A butcher. At *macelleria* in larger towns and cities, you may need to take a numbered ticket and wait to be called before you are served.

From left: A Verona *salumeria*; Mercato della Vucciria, Palermo

MERCATO

Meaning simply 'market'. However, if you ask for '*Il mercato*', you'll probably be pointed in the direction of a supermarket.

NORCINERIA

Specialist pork butchers – they take their name from the Umbrian town of Norcia, which is renowned for its pork butchers.

PASTICCERIA

A bakery selling pastries, biscuits, cakes and desserts. Each city and each region serves their own specialities.

PASTIFICIO

A specialist pasta shop, usually making and selling *pasta fresca* (fresh pasta) as well as gnocchi.

PESCHERIA

Specialist fish shop or market, selling all kinds of seafood.

POLLERIA

Poultry (*pollame*) shop, which might stock anything from guinea fowl and chicken to quail and pheasant.

SALUMERIA

Salumerie sell a range of meat products such as prosciutto, salami, *salsicce* (sausages) and the like. Products can be sliced according to your needs.

SUPERMERCATO

A supermarket. Often shortened, rather confusingly, to simply '*mercato*'.

TABACCHI

Shops that sell tobacco, as well as magazines, newspapers, sweets, bus/train tickets and other small items. Many bars are also *tabacchi*.

TORREFAZIONE

Coffee roastery where you can buy ground and unground beans directly after roasting.

MARKET RULES

DON'T BE SHY
Enquire about what is good, fresh or just arrived; you'll usually find you're offered a taste of the produce on offer. The chatting is part of the process and often results in a discount.

DON'T TOUCH THE GOODS
Manhandling prime produce is a no-no. Instead, point to the thing you're interested in and tell the stallholder when you'd like to eat it, so they can choose the appropriate item.

LEARN HOW TO QUEUE WITHOUT QUEUEING
If a stall is busy, assess who's next and make eye contact with the vendor. In the morning, you'll need to mind sharp-elbowed *nonnas* (grandmothers) who have a knack of always being served first.

AT THE MARKET

The market (*mercato*) sits at the heart of every Italian town and city. Big or small, held daily, weekly or monthly, the market is an Italian tradition that has been fostered over centuries, and you'll find every section of Italian society shopping here.

Large cities and towns like Padua, Bologna and Naples host daily markets; smaller towns and villages stage them twice-weekly or weekly. Most start trading at 7am and finish at 1pm, Monday to Saturday. Hot food stands and refrigerated mobile carts specialising in cheese, meat and fish sit alongside fruit and veg stalls, and often there are seeds, flowers, tools, pots, pans, linen and clothing on sale as well.

Good markets are a total revelation. While there is very little difference in price between shop- and market-bought food, there is a huge difference in quality and freshness. A reputable stallholder will not only tell you which fruit and vegetables are in season, but also how to cook them. And if they really care, they may even slip in extras like a bundle of mixed herbs with your purchases.

ITALY'S TOP 10 FOOD MARKETS

EATALY, TURIN

The original Slow Food emporium offers a staggering array of organic, sustainable food and drink, from fresh produce to local delicacies.

IL SALONE, PADUA

Europe's oldest covered market, set beneath the arches of a Gothic palazzo.

MERCATO DI RIALTO, VENICE

The commercial heart of Venice for 1000 years, selling unique fish and seafood from the lagoon and around Italy.

MERCATO DI MEZZO, BOLOGNA

A three-storey gourmet food hall where you can buy pizza, craft beer, cheese and charcuterie.

MERCATO DI PIAZZA CAMPO DEL PALIO, ASTI

A twice-weekly market in a vast piazza, offering Piedmontese specialities like mushrooms, truffles and red apples.

MERCATO DI SANT'AMBROGIO, FLORENCE

Off the beaten-path, the stalls at Sant'Ambrogio sell the finest organic produce in Tuscany.

NUOVO MERCATO DI TESTACCIO, ROME

A vast, 5000-sq-metre structure hosting hundreds of stalls, from food to fashion. It's also a great place for lunch.

LA PESCHERIA, NAPLES

The oldest of 60 Neapolitan markets, Pignasecca is raucous, fun and full of stunning produce and fish.

BALLARÒ MARKET, PALERMO

Full of noisy vendors, this ancient market sells seasonal delicacies like fresh ricotta and heirloom tomatoes.

LA PISCHERIA, CATANIA

A historic fish market in the black lava-built town of Catania. The constant calls of vendors (*vuciata*) lend a souk-like vibe.

DRiNKS

Right: In Italy, a meal without wine is like pasta without sauce

COFFEE

Clockwise from top left: Il Caffe Rosso, Venice; A *marocchino* (an espresso with cocoa powder); Caffè Florian, Venice

Given their love of the bean, you might think that Italians invented coffee. They didn't. Coffee is native to East Africa, and the first records of it being roasted and drunk come from Sufi shrines in the Yemen during the 15th century.

But ever since the so-called 'wine of the Arabs' reached Venice in the 17th century, the Italian passion for coffee has generated a culture unrivalled anywhere else in the world, and which now underpins a hugely valuable industry.

After all, it was an Italian, Angelo Moriondo, who first patented a steam-powered coffee machine. His prototype was further refined by Luigi Bezzera and Desiderio Pavoni, who presented the world's first espresso (the word means 'made on the spur of the moment') machine at the 1906 Milan Fair. Roughly the same technology still exists in today's coffeeshop apparatus, although it took a further 40 years before Milanese café owner Achille Gaggia developed his lever-operated machine with spring-piston pressure, which did away with the need for large boilers, standardised the size of the cups and enabled the creation of the signature *crema*, the amber froth that tops a good espresso.

Aside from the technology and design, there is an art to making coffee that is distinctly Italian too. The talent of the barista is as important as the quality of the beans and the reliability of the machine. A good espresso depends on the four M's: *macchina*, the machine; *macinazione*, the proper grinding of the beans (a uniform grind between fine and powdery is required); *miscela*, the coffee blend and roast; and *mano*, the skilled hand of the barista.

But while Italian coffee consumption is sustained by rituals that embed, fortify and refine familiar habits and rituals, this adherence to tradition and a failure to keep pace with changing lifestyles and attitudes has seen Italy's dominance as the world's leading coffee culture sorely tested. Swiss firm Nestlé has stolen a march on the market for personal espresso-makers with its Nespresso system, while in 2018, American coffeehouse Starbucks opened its first Reserve Roastery in Milan, offering coffee alongside a 'lifestyle experience' in a beautiful premises.

Antonio Baravalle, CEO of family-owned, Turin-based coffeehouse Lavazza, sees the arrival of Starbucks as a positive opportunity. He believes that challenge and innovation have always been part of the Italian identity, and sees Starbucks' entry to the country's coffee scene as a wake-up call to the local market. In anticipation, both Lavazza and Illycaffe have opened

flagship cafés in Milan. And in 2018, Lavazza unveiled a 30,000-sq-metre, eco-conscious Turin HQ that incorporates a coffee museum, landscaped gardens and an archaeological area displaying a 4th-century basilica.

Meanwhile, a new wave of Italian coffee aficionados have answered the challenge of the latest 'third wave' speciality coffee movement, which specifically rejects Italy's signature multi-bean blends and dark roasts in favour of artisanal, single-origin roasts. Award-winning roasters like Rubens Gardelli and Davide Cobelli (the latter is head trainer at Verona's Coffee Training Academy) see an exciting opportunity in the job of re-educating palates to the extraordinary range of fruity flavours presented by single-origin beans. Seek out similar third-wave pioneers at Faro in Rome, Estratto in Brescia, Orsonero in Milan, Ditta Artigianale in Florence and Orso Laboratorio Caffè in Turin.

COFFEE CULTURE

Think of your first Italian coffee order as an unofficial initiation ceremony. Rule number one: don't ask for a large double-shot, skinny vanilla latte. Most Italian coffee orders can be made by uttering a single word: 'caffè'. This is a single shot of espresso (the term 'espresso' is rarely used in Italian coffee-bar parlance).

A macchiato is an espresso with a dash of steamed milk, while an Americano is an espresso with added hot water, making for a slightly longer drink. The king of all white coffees is the cappuccino, an espresso topped with warm frothy milk with an optional sprinkling of chocolate.

All coffee in Italy is served at the perfect temperature for flavour – that's *tiepido* (tepid). This means that the *crema*, that rich, caramel-coloured foam on top of an espresso, preserves the aroma without being bitter. It also means that any milk is heated with steam to create a thick, rich, dense and wet foam (*schiuma*) that captures the essence of the *crema*. If you don't like your coffee at this temperature, then you ask for it *'molto caldo'* (very hot).

Similarly, there are no size differentials in Italy. The humongous half-litre (20oz) latte – a staple drink in North America – could caffeinate a whole business meeting in Rome. The standard cappuccino

comes in a 180mL (6oz) porcelain cup. Low-fat milk is rarely available, although soya milk is becoming more common. Most places serve decaf but, if not, opt for a caffeine-free, barley-based *orzo* instead. Take care when ordering lattes. The word *latte* means milk in Italian; order one and that's what you'll get. A *caffè latte* is a glass of warm milk with a tiny droplet of coffee in it.

Takeaway drinks are noticeably absent from the Italian coffee scene. Except in train stations, cafés rarely stock disposable take-out cups. Hurry or no hurry, you'll be expected to prop up the bar with the locals, or – for a slight premium – perch at a tiny table. Likewise, Italian bars don't offer instant coffee, ever. Interestingly, espresso contains less caffeine than instant or percolated coffee.

Traditionally, a cappuccino is taken in the morning. Some people suggest that it's a massive faux pas to order one after 11am, but while it's unlikely that your Italian friends will be sticking milk in their coffee after lunch, afternoon and late-night cappuccino-drinking is not – as yet – an illegal activity. Just make sure you apologise first.

In bars, coffee is often served with a small glass of water, which is supposed to be drunk first to cleanse the palate. In busy bars (especially in train stations), you must pay for your coffee upfront at a till and then present your receipt to the barista. Italian coffee is also refreshingly cheap: a cup shouldn't cost more than €1–2.

REGIONAL VARIATIONS

Although simple is generally best, Italian coffee has a surprising amount of regional variation. The *bicerin* is a speciality of Piedmont, particularly Turin, and has been around for at least 200 years. It consists of layered espresso, hot chocolate and milk, and is served in a glass. Not dissimilar is the *marocchino*, another Piedmontese invention, a mix of espresso, cocoa powder and milk froth.

In Trentino, a *cappuccino Viennese* is a frothy coffee with chocolate and cinnamon. In Le Marche, stop for a *caffè anisette* and you'll get an aniseed-flavoured espresso; in Sicily, you'll find *caffè d'u parrinu*, coffee flavoured with cloves, cinnamon and cocoa powder. Other regional rituals around coffee include the Neapolitan practice of *caffè sospeso* (a 'suspended' coffee), whereby you pay for two coffees but leave one for a stranger to enjoy for free.

As one of the first major purveyors of coffee in Europe, Trieste has a unique coffee culture and even a lexicon of its own. If you're after an espresso in Trieste, order a *nero*; for a macchiato, it's a *capo*, and when you want a cappuccino, request a *caffelatte*. However, if you ask for a *nero* elsewhere, you may well end up with a glass of red wine!

Right: Espresso is known simply as *caffè*
Below: Serving coffee at a cafe in Turin

ITALY'S BEST COFFEE CiTiES

TRIESTE

Home of Illy coffee and still one of Europe's major coffee-processing ports. Full of roasteries and historic coffeehouses such as Caffè degli Specchi (1839), Caffè Tommaseo (1830) and Caffè San Marco (1914).

MILAN

Where the espresso machine was born, and where you'll find the historic coffeehouses Caffè Cova (1817), Caffè Savini (1867), Caffè Biffi (1887) and Camparino (1915).

TURIN

The city of the moka pot and of Lavazza, Turin is where the idea of an Italian nation was born, in coffeehouses like Al Bicerin (1763), Caffè Platti (1875) and Caffè Mulassano (1907).

NAPLES

An upholder of tradition, where most baristas still use lever machines and maintain customs like boiling the cups. The city's most famous café is Gambrinus (1860).

Coffee Decoder

CAFFÈ
While the word means coffee, it always implies espresso if used alone.

CAFFÈ CORRETTO
An espresso with a drop of alcohol (usually grappa) added to 'correct' it.

CAFFÈ DECAFFEINATO
Decaffeinated coffee.

CAFFÈ FREDDO
A shot of coffee in cold milk, drunk in the south in summer.

CAFFÈ LATTE
A milkier version of the cappuccino, with less foam.

CAFFÈ LUNGO
(Doppio, Americano). A long coffee. This means 'double' but it's usually made with a single shot of coffee with extra water poured through.

CAFFÈ MACCHIATO
An espresso 'stained' with a dash of milk. You can order it *caldo* (with hot milk), or *freddo* (with cold milk).

CAPPUCCINO
A shot of espresso, topped with foamed milk and sometimes dusted with cocoa; a favourite Italian breakfast.

LATTE MACCHIATO
Warmed milk 'stained' with a shot of coffee, usually served in a long glass.

MACCHIATONE
A bigger version of a *caffè macchiato caldo*, but without as much milk or foam as a cappuccino.

RISTRETTO
A 'restricted' coffee. The essence of the bean – the machine's first dribble, strong but not bitter.

Mineral Water & SOFT DRINKS

MINERAL WATER

Italy is one of the world's leading producers and consumers of mineral water (*acqua minerale*), producing nearly 12% of the world's supply and getting through nearly twice the European average. Alongside wine, water is an essential staple of any Italian table. As soon as you sit down in a restaurant you'll be asked if you want *frizzante/gassata* or *naturale* (sparkling/carbonated or still) water.

The two main drivers behind the consumption of mineral water are health and taste. Mineral waters are marketed as hygienic, healthy and full of nutrients. Many older Italians think drinking tap water (*acqua potabili*) is unsanitary, even though Italian tap water adheres to high international health standards. That said, Italian water is hard and full of calcium, which can result in a slightly chalky taste.

There are hundreds of branded mineral waters in Italy, some of the most famous being San Pellegrino, Acqua Panna, San Benedetto,

Ferrarelle and Levissima. By law, they must be drawn from an underground source and many are naturally slightly carbonated, which Italians tend to prefer.

These days, however, people are increasingly concerned about the plastic waste that the mineral water industry generates, and many restaurants in bigger cities

are installing water filtration systems. Likewise, fee-charging stations dispensing filtered water are also popping up. In addition, most Italian cities are dotted with water fountains which provide clean, drinkable water for free. It's also perfectly fine to ask for tap water (*acqua del rubinetto*) in a restaurant.

Left: Making soft drinks in summer.
From top: Drinking fountains dot Italian cities; Regional fruit is used in drinks; Water is a staple of any Italian table

SOFT DRINKS

While you can find all the big soft drink brands – Coca-Cola, Pepsi, Fanta and Sprite – in Italy, Italians aren't big consumers of sweet sodas. In fact, they drink around 40L (8.8 gallons) per head each year, far below the European average of 67L (14.7 gallons).

Since the invention of soda water in 1767, Italian companies have used regional fruit to make a range of home-grown soft drinks. Typically these are not as sweet as their Western counterparts, and usually come in tiny bottles. Some of the most common are listed below:

ARANCIATA The classic Italian orange drink with an intense orange flavour thanks to its base of Sicilian blood oranges. Aranciata Amara is a bitter version, while Limonata is the lemon version.

CEDRATA TASSONI One of the oldest soft drinks in Italy, initially marketed as a health syrup and now derived from the lemon-like *diamante* citrus from Calabria.

CHINOTTO The homegrown version of cola, this dark, lightly herbaceous drink with a slightly bitter taste is made from the sour fruit of the myrtle-leaved orange tree grown along the Ligurian Riviera. After a period in decline, it's now regaining its popularity.

COLA BALADIN Another cola-style drink, this time made from the West African kola nut, which comes from the same family as cocoa and contains caffeine.

CRODINO A soft drink that doubles as an *aperitivo*, this orange-coloured soda has a light fizz and a good mix of sweetness and bitterness.

GAZOSSA Italian-style lemonade made using *sfusato* lemons from the Amalfi Coast, a variety that was saved from extinction by Slow Food campaigners.

SANBITTÈR Bitter, red-coloured soft drink that's popular as a non-alcoholic alternative to Campari during *aperitivo*.

Right: Tasting beers in the historical Rione Monti district

CRAFT BEER

Who comes to Italy for beer? Not many people, and few realise just how dynamic Italy's craft beer (*birre artigianali*) scene is, or have ever heard of any of the hundreds of artisanal lagers, ales and beers on offer.

This is hardly surprising, given the dominance of the great beer-making countries to the north, the preference of Italians themselves for wine and the fact that the country's craft beer movement only really kicked off in 1996, when Teo Musso founded the Birreria

Baladin in Piozzo, Piedmont, and Agostino Arioli opened Birrificio Italiano in Lombardy.

Today, craft beer is going from strength to strength, with over 1000 craft breweries, microbreweries and brewpubs producing quality products that are gaining global recognition through events like the European Beer Star contest. Young Italians are increasingly adopting the habit of going out to a bar, pub or microbrewery for a beer, and beer remains the most popular accompaniment to pizza. That said, Italian drinkers are still Europe's lowest per-capita consumers of beer.

ITALIAN CRAFT BEERS

To be considered 'craft', Italian beer must be unfiltered and unpasteurized, and come from a brewery that makes fewer than 170,000 barrels a year. Most Italian breweries, however, are much, much smaller than this, and many of them are concentrated in the north, particularly in and around Milan and in the Veneto.

Like Italian wines, the most interesting craft beers are closely tied to the territory in which they're produced. Passionate brewers utilise heirloom grains, malt types, local fruits, nuts, spices and herbs – even clams. In addition, because there are so few historic beer styles in Italy, brewers here are free to be creative and combine the best aspects of Belgian, British, German and American brewing traditions and techniques. This results in an astonishing diversity of styles and flavours.

The only officially recognised Italian beer style is Grape Ale, a sort of fruit beer with wine added at the fermentation stage. Unofficially, though, there are dozens of Italian beer styles, from winter and Halloween beers to stout, golden ale, Scotch ale and India pale ale; there are also white, wheat, chestnut, honey and even tea beers.

Like local wines, the best of these beers are crafted to express the terroir and can only be found in local pubs and bars. They may be served in artful glass bottles or in a smaller wine-like goblet called a TeKu (a mash-up of Teo and Kuaska, the two Italian beer aficionados who created it), which is designed to capture and release the beer's aromas. The TeKu's smaller size also keeps cost down – beer-brewing, unlike winemaking, isn't subsidized in Italy, so craft beer is relatively expensive in comparison (a 33cL/11oz bottle costs €5.50–€6.50 in Milan and Rome).

BEERS TO LOOK OUT FOR

BEERBERA (LoverBeer)
A sour ale employing wild fermentation of freshly pressed Barbera grapes to achieve a hazy red colour and a tart taste, full of the flavour of sour cherry and blueberry.

PERLE AI PORCI (Birra del Borgo) *Inspired by British and Nordic traditions, this oyster stout has Fine de Claire oysters (shells and all) added during the boil.*

QUARTA RUNA (Birrificio Montegioco)
With a nod to Belgian ales, Montegioco produces sophisticated fruit beers like Quarta Runa, a pale ale brewed with baked Volpedo peaches.

TIPOPILS (Birrificio Italiano)
A pilsner-like beer which employs four types of Czech and German hops, and expertly blends the bitterness of the hops with the sweetness of the malt.

XYAUYÙ (Birreria Baladin)
A line of vintage barley wines that undergo a process of controlled oxidization that gives a rich, caramel taste.

WINE

Italy is the world's largest producer of wine (*vino*), and while quantity isn't any measure of excellence, the quality and diversity of Italian wines are also second to none.

Italian winemakers can draw on an enviable depth of knowledge that spans nearly 4000 years, and the country's wildly varied terroir and multiple microclimates have led to an extraordinary level of creativity and inventiveness.

In Italy, wine isn't just a drink: it represents history, culture, geography and identity. Each great bottle of wine is a capsule of time, terroir and vintage to be savoured and contemplated. As a result, a sit-down meal without wine in Italy is as unpalatable as pasta without sauce. Not ordering wine at a restaurant can cause consternation – are you pregnant? Was it something the waiter said?

Here, wine is a consideration as essential as your choice of dinner date. Indeed, while the country's perfectly quaffable pilsner beers and occasional craft ale pair well with roast meats, pizza and other quick eats, vino is considered the only appropriate accompaniment for a proper meal – and since many wines cost less than a pint in Italy, this is not a question of price, but a matter of flavour.

Italian wines are considered among the most versatile and 'food friendly' in the world, specifically cultivated over the centuries to elevate regional cuisine. Some will be as familiar

DRINKING & DRIVING

The legal limit for blood-alcohol when driving is 0.05%; it's zero for drivers under 21 and those who have had a licence for less than three years. Random breath tests are conducted.

to you as old flames, including pizza-and-a-movie Chianti or reliable summertime fling Pinot Grigio. But you'll also find some captivating Italian varietals and blends for which there is no translation (such as Brunello di Montalcino, Vermentino or Sciacchetrà), and intriguing Italian wines that have little in common with European and New World cousins of the same name, from Merlot and Pinot Nero (aka Pinot Noir) to Chardonnay.

Many visitors default to carafes of house reds or whites, which in Italy usually means young, fruit-forward reds to complement tomato sauces and chilled, dry whites as seafood palate-cleansers. But with a little daring, you can pursue a wider range of options by the glass or half-bottle, and any Italian sommelier worth their salt will be thrilled to guide you.

WINE CONSUMPTION

The average Italian adult drinks around 34L (7.8 gallons) of wine per annum – a sobering figure compared with the 100L (23 gallons) consumed on average back in the 1950s. Somewhat surprisingly, the world's top consumers of wine per person live in the Vatican City, where the average amount is 54L (12 gallons) per year.

ITALIAN WINEMAKING THROUGH THE AGES

Italy has a hugely rich viticultural heritage. Both the Etruscans and Greeks (who incorporated much of southern Italy into Magna Graecia) cultivated vines from the wild Vitis Vinifera grape from about 800 BCE onwards, making Italy one of the world's first wine-producing territories. Growing grapes in Italy was so easy, in fact, that the Greeks named the area Oenotria, or 'Land of Wine'.

But it wasn't until the 2nd century BCE, when the Romans established their great farms and vineyards, that Italian winemaking methods evolved to support large-scale production. Wine was so valuable as a commodity that the Romans initially outlawed viticulture outside of Italy; instead, they traded wine for slaves, who were then put to work in the vineyards to produce more wine. Only over time was this prohibition relaxed, allowing vineyards to flourish in the rest of Europe, particularly in Gaul (present-day France) and Hispania (Spain).

Roman wine was young, strong and unrefined (and probably oxidized), so it was typically mixed with water, honey or spices before drinking. But although we no longer share the Romans' taste in wine, the legacy of their winemaking processes deserves plenty of appreciation. They improved upon the Greek wine presses,

ROMANS **LOVED WINE** *and drank it* **IN VAST** QUANTITIES

introduced the trellis as a means to train vines, figured out which wines thrived in different climates and invented wooden barrels in order to age vintages. They might also have been the first to use corked glass jars for storage.

It's fair to say that Romans loved wine. They drank it in vast quantities to celebrate feast days and festivals, and particularly for Bacchanalia, the feast honouring the god of wine, Bacchus. These parties were so wild that they were eventually banned by the Roman Senate.

The rise of Christianity in the 4th century CE changed the Italian relationship with wine forever. Wine became part of the Holy Sacrament and, as a result, became ennobled. Medieval monks took up viticulture and set about codifying it, experimenting with new vinification techniques, growing methods and hybridisation. As monastic land was protected, the heritage vines they grew were also protected, and winemaking thrived throughout the Middle Ages and Renaissance.

Then, in the 19th century, along with much of Europe, the vine louse phylloxera destroyed many of Italy's ancient vineyards. In the vast replanting efforts, vineyards were designed for

quantity rather than quality and Italian winemaking took a nosedive. Italy became synonymous with cheap table wines of poor quality. In fact, much of the full-bodied red wine from the country's south was used as a base for more refined French wine.

In the 1960s, the Italian government responded to this perilous state of affairs by establishing the DOC (Denominazione di Origine Controllata) quality control system, which introduced strict winemaking regulations and accredited labelling. Since then, Italian wines have gone from strength to strength, finally regaining recognition on the world stage thanks to pioneering Tuscan vintners in the 1980s. Even more recently, a re-evaluation of the country's rich patrimony of indigenous grapes has begun. This exciting renaissance promises to unlock the potential of indigenous grapes like Nero d'Avola, Fiano, Sagrantino, Vitovska and Teroldego that are unique to Italy.

Above: A cart delivers wine in Tuscany in the 1920s

WINE CLASSIFICATION

To ensure quality control, Italy has a highly specific classification system which takes into account geographical area, grape varietals, ageing requirements and other winemaking controls. The basic Italian quality designations are DOCG, DOC and IGT. Anything that does not fit into these categories is classified *vino da tavola* (table wine), without the right to include a vintage, place name or grape variety on the label.

DOCG

DENOMINATION OF CONTROLLED AND GUARANTEED ORIGIN

Wines in this category guarantee the best quality and are made according to the highest standards, dictating everything from permitted yield limits to winemaking techniques and bottling. The classification was introduced in 1963, but the first DOCG wine wasn't approved until 1980. In 2019, there were only 74 DOCG wines, the majority of which are made in Piedmont, Veneto and Tuscany.

• Wine must demonstrate the characteristics of a small territory
• Grapes and wine must be produced within the area of origin
• Wines are subject to physical and chemical analysis and go through two expert tastings before being given DOCG status
• Wines are made according to the most traditional methods possible

DOC

DENOMINATION OF CONTROLLED ORIGIN

This is the main tier of Italian wine classification and is equivalent to the French Appellation d'Origine Contrôlée (AOC). Wines in this category are still highly regulated, but not as stringently as DOCG wines. In 2019, there were 329 DOC wines – Chianti, Barolo and Amarone di Valpolicella all appear in this category.

• Wine must demonstrate the characteristics of a larger area than DOCG wines
• Grapes and wine must be produced within the area of origin
• Wines are subject to a single chemical and physical analysis and one tasting before being approved
• Wines are typically made according to the territory's traditional methods

IGT

PROTECTED GEOGRAPHICAL INDICATION

This classification was created in 1992 in response to the criticism that the restrictions of the DOC system were inhibiting experimentation and creativity in winemaking. Therefore, IGT allows winemakers more flexibility without compromising quality, which is why IGT wines are often organic, biodynamic and natural varieties. Although IGT is technically considered a step below DOC, you'll still find some of the country's best wines in this category.

• Grapes and wine still need to be produced within an area of origin, but it is larger than for the DOC
• Wines are subject to analysis but not to tasting, as the flavour can vary between vintages or even bottles
• Includes 'Super Tuscans', as they include non-indigenous grape varieties such as Merlot, Cabernet Sauvignon and Syrah

SUPER TUSCANS

'Super Tuscan' is a term that emerged in the 1980s to describe high quality red wines from Tuscany made using a blend of non-indigenous wine grape. The first Super Tuscan, Tignanello, was created by the Antinori winery in 1971 from a blend of 80% Sangiovese, 15% Cabernet Sauvignon and 5% Cabernet Franc grapes. As Super Tuscan wines were made using unsanctioned grapes, they could not be recognized by the DOC classification system and, therefore, ended up in the vino da tavola category – despite being lauded in international markets. Eventually, the classification system adapted in 1992 with the creation of the IGT category – all Super Tuscans now have a Toscana IGT classification.

Roman times and produces a huge range of wines, from champagne-style Franciacorta and fizzy-red Lambrusco to bombastic Sforzato and intense, spicy Nebbiolo (also called Chiavennasca here), alongside considerable volumes of Pinot Nero, Pinot Grigio, Chardonnay, Cabernet and Sauvignon. Still, Piedmont is by far the most important wine region of the northwest, home to the fruity, Beaujolais-style Dolcetto, the smoothly tannic Barbera, the peachy white Arneis and the world-famous Barolo and Barbaresco, which are made from 100% Nebbiolo grapes grown in the clay and limestone terroir around Alba.

GRAPE VARIETIES

Wine is made in all 20 regions of Italy, ranging across latitudes from the 38th parallel (near Tunisia) in Sicily to the 45th parallel (near Burgundy, France) in the mountainous north, and across altitudes, from under 10m (33ft) below sea level to more than 1000m (3300ft) above. Across this huge geographic and climatic variation, Italy harvests some 700 commercially used grape varieties.

Within Italy there are four distinctive macro zones: the northwest, which has maintained quality principles longest; the northeast, which has the best blend of traditional and modern techniques and tastes; the centre, which is the heart of the modern Italian

wine renaissance; and the south, which is the most traditional.

NORTHWEST ITALY

The four regions of Piedmont, Liguria, Lombardy and the Valle d'Aosta make up this zone, which borders France and Switzerland. In the Valle d'Aosta, you'll find subalpine-style wines from French or French-sounding varieties such as Blanc de Morgex, Gamay, Pinot Noir and Fumin. Liguria is basically an extension of the French Riviera, and produces mainly white wines based on crisp Vermentino grapes as well as a Passito (dried-grape wine) from the rare indigenous Sciacchetrà grape.

Lombardy has been in the business of winemaking since

NORTHEAST ITALY

The extraordinary variety of wines from Italy's three northeastern regions of Trentino Alto Adige, Friuli Venezia Giulia and Veneto are a result of the area's dramatic landscape. Trentino is entirely alpine and supports a broad mix of Gallic and Germanic grape varieties such as Pinot Bianco, Riesling, Traminer and Grüner Veltliner. Look out for beautiful aromatic whites such as Gewürztraminer, well-structured reds derived from indigenous Schiava and Lagrein grapes and sturdier winter warmers

employing Cabernet and the tannic Terolego.

Underrated Friuli produces some stunning wines that are rarely seen outside the region. They are conjured from local grape varieties such as red Refosco, sweet Picolit, apricot-like Friulano and sharp, dry, red Schioppettino. Still, it is the Veneto that dominates winemaking here, boasting three of Italy's most famous wines: light, bright Prosecco, personable but complex Soave, derived from the Garganega grape, and the intensely cherry-tasting Valpolicella, which ranges from a medium-weight, quaffable table red to deep, rich, bitter-cherry Amarone and jammy, port-like Recioto.

Above: Customers weigh their options at a bar in Venice

CENTRAL ITALY

While white wines generally predominate in the mountainous north of the country, the warmer Mediterranean climate of central Italy is better suited to reds. Of all the native grapes here, it is Sangiovese that dominates, and the most famous of these are undoubtedly the spicy and complex wines made in Montalcino and Montepulciano. Lighter and friendlier is the internationally recognised Chianti Classico, made from a blend of Sangiovese, Canaiolo and up to 20% of any other approved red grape variety.

The newly DOCG-certified Gran Selezione sits at the top of the Chianti quality pyramid.

Otherwise, varieties like Cabernet Sauvignon, Cabernet Franc, Merlot and Syrah do well in this region, alongside interesting indigenous varieties such as Umbria's complex and tannic Sagrantino and Abruzzo's Cerasuolo. Red is so dominant in the Central region that whites simply can't compete on quality. That said, the Verdicchio variety from the central Apennines is one of Italy's most versatile white grapes, and San Gimignano's ancient Vernaccia (grown here since the 13th century and the second white in Italy to achieve DOCG status), Abruzzo's Pecorino and Lazio's aromatic Frascati are all worth sampling.

THE SOUTH

Southern Italy represents a vast portion of the country, covering the regions of Campania, Calabria, Basilicata and Puglia, as well as the islands of Sicily and Sardinia. It is hot and arid, and dotted with active volcanoes (Vesuvius, Etna and Stromboli) as well as some significant mountain peaks. Thanks to its diversity, the area boasts an interesting variety of grapes, producing some very complex, robust reds suitable for long ageing, as well as some very notable sweet wines.

Given its broad, flat expanses, Puglia is the south's largest wine-producing region, rivalling the Veneto in its quantity of wines. The

Montepulciano grape can also be found here, but the two most distinctive native varieties are Primitivo, a cousin of California's Zinfandel, that delivers strong, Port-style wines; and Negroamaro, literally summing up the taste as 'black-bitter'.

Sicily and Sardinia also turn out some great reds. In Sicily, the local hero is the Nero d'Avola grape, which produces fruity, medium-bodied wines; and Grillo, which makes for peachy whites. In Sardinia, it is Carignano and Cannonau (aka Grenache) reds and the crisp, almost salty Vermentino white. Given the high sugar content of many southern grapes, sweet wines are also prominent, most famously Sicily's Marsala, a fortified wine made from the white Grillo grape that comes in dry and sweet varieties. There's also honey-sweet Malvasia from the Aeolian Islands and the fabled Moscato di Pantelleria, a benchmark Moscato made from Zibibbo grapes with a delicious floral bouquet and a delightful apricot taste.

Campania, too, has the outstanding red Aglianico, which thrives in the Apennines and is thought to be Italy's oldest cultivated grape. Taurasi, produced in the high hills east of Avellino, is the best of these – it's sometimes called the Barolo of the south for its dark berry, leather and roasted-coffee notes. Thanks to the fertile slopes of Vesuvius, Campania is also the only southern region with a wealth of white wines, derived here from grapes such as Falanghina, Fiano and Greco. In the province of Caserta, look out for Falerno del Massico, a DOC-designated wine hailing from the very same area as Falernum, the most celebrated wine of ancient Roman times.

VIN SANTO

Vin Santo's name literally translates as 'holy wine', indicating that it may have been used in the Catholic ritual of mass at some point. Traditionally a sipping wine, it's made from semi-dried Trebbiano Toscano, Malvasia and Grechetto grapes, which are pressed and sealed in caratelli (small barrels) for three years. The wine varies from sweet to semi-sweet and dry. It's usually golden-amber in colour and beautifully aromatic, and, at its best, Vin Santo is one of Italy's finest dessert wines.

WINE STYLES

Italy has all the familiar wine styles, plus a few more besides. The frizzante sparkling wines include those made in the French-style *metodo tradizionale* (champagne method) manner. These are often referred to as spumante, the word spuma referencing the froth that arises as they're poured. The most famous of the fizzies is Moscato d'Asti (no longer allowed to be called Spumante), and the Veneto's Prosecco. Prosecco Brut is a spumante, but it's as dry as any sparkling wine.

By far the most common wines in Italy, reds are known as *vino rosso*; whites are *vino bianco* and rosé-style wines *vino rosato*. Along with these, you'll find vino da contemplazione/meditazione (wines of contemplation/meditation). This term is often applied to great, structured wines such as Brunello di Montalcino and Barolo, or to sweet, complex dessert wines, which don't need to be paired with food but can and should be savoured alone. One sweet meditazione wine, hailing from the Sicilian island of Pantelleria, is the Passito di Pantelleria, a surprisingly lush yet not overly sweet wine with a length and character that is not really suited to dessert, or to the meal proper. It's more suited to sipping while sitting around and contemplating life and all its pleasures.

Passito di Pantelleria is made using the *passito* method, an ancient and distinguishing feature of Italian wine that dates to pre-Classical times. Under this classic method, grapes are harvested and then laid out to dry (instead of being crushed), traditionally on straw mats and more recently on wooden racks (a process called *appasimento*). The resulting grapes tend to raisin, drying out and going mouldy in the process and causing the juice within to condense and sweeten. Passito wines tend to be sweet to very sweet whites, such as the Malvasia delle Lipari Passito, Tuscany's Vin Santo and Friuli's Verduzzo Friulano. However, some aren't sweet at all, the most famous example being the Veneto's Amarone della Valpolicella, a ripe, raisiny red wine with very little acid. If fermentation is incomplete, the result is a sweet red wine called Recioto; the white Recioto di Soave is a very old, sweet white wine often drunk with panettone at Christmas.

ESSENTIAL WINE PRIMER

SPARKLING WINES
Franciacorta (Lombardy), Prosecco (Veneto), Asti (Piedmont), Lambrusco (Emilia-Romagna)

LIGHT, CITRUSY WHITES WITH GRASSY OR FLORAL NOTES
Vermentino (Sardinia), Orvieto (Umbria), Soave (Veneto), Tocai (Friuli), Frascati (Lazio)

DRY WHITES WITH AROMATIC HERBAL OR MINERAL ASPECTS
Cinque Terre (Liguria), Lugana (southern Lake Garda), Gavi (Piedmont), Falanghina (Campania), Est! Est!! Est!!! (Lazio)

VERSATILE, FOOD-FRIENDLY REDS WITH PLEASANT ACIDITY
Barbera d'Alba (Piedmont), Montepulciano d'Abruzzo (Abruzzo), Valpolicella (Veneto), Chianti Classico (Tuscany), Bardolino (Lombardy), Sangiovese (Tuscany)

WELL-ROUNDED REDS, BALANCING FRUIT WITH EARTHY NOTES
Brunello di Montalcino (Tuscany), Refosco dal Peduncolo (Friuli), Dolcetto (Piedmont), Morellino di Scansano (Tuscany), Oltrepò Pavese (Lombardy)

BIG, STRUCTURED REDS WITH VELVETY TANNINS
Amarone (Veneto), Barolo (Piedmont), Sagrantino di Montefalco (Umbria), Sassicaia and other 'Super-Tuscan' blends (Tuscany)

FORTIFIED AND DESSERT WINES
Sciacchetrà (Liguria), Colli Orientali del Friuli Picolit (Friuli), Vin Santo (Tuscany), Moscato d'Asti (Piedmont)

From top: A Tuscan grape harvest; Red wine in Rome

WINE & FOOD PAIRINGS

Italian wines are extremely well balanced and pair well with a wide variety of food. When deciding what to drink, always consider the characteristics of the region you are in. Take note of the vegetables, herbs and spices used, and remember that the produce on your plate is grown in the same soil as the grapes in your wine, so will have complementary flavours. If in doubt, simply follow the old adage: 'if it grows together, it goes together.'

WHITE WINES

SPARKLING WHITE WINES

Brut Spumante, Moscato d'Asti, Prosecco and Franciacorta are all popular aperitifs drunk with or without *antipasti*.

DRY WHITE WINES

Pinot Grigio, Gavi, Soave, Arneis, Fiano di Avellino, Friulano and Vermentino can also be drunk with *antipasti*, as well as with shellfish, crustaceans, fish and pesto pastas.

MEDIUM-BODIED WHITE WINES

Chardonnay, Friulano, Müller Thurgau, Malvasia, Greco di Tufo and Etna Bianco pair well with creamy pastas and risottos, spicy seafood, fried *antipasti*, bean-based dishes, chicken and charcuterie.

RED WINES

SWEET WINES

SPARKLING RED WINES

Served slightly chilled and enjoyed while young, sparkling reds like Lambrusco and Bardolino Chiaretto pair well with charcuterie (salumi), as their fresh and acidic character cuts through the fat. They also go well with shellfish and plates of parmesan drizzled with balsamic.

LIGHT RED WINES

Bardolino, Dolcetto, Montepulciano d'Abruzzo, Valpolicella and entry-level Chianti can be served with chicken, delicate beef dishes (such as tagliata di manzo, sliced fillet), veal, and pasta with red or light pork-based sauces.

MEDIUM–BODIED RED WINES

Barbera, Merlot, Nebbiolo, Rosso di Montalcino, Sangiovese and Sagrantino all go well with pork, beef, lamb, turkey, duck and goose, as well as with mushrooms, red-meat risottos, pizzas with tomato and meat sauces and sheep's milk cheeses. Sicily's medium-bodied, plummy Nero d'Avola will also pair wonderfully with spicy couscous and fish dishes that incorporate the island's flavourful tuna or swordfish.

FULL–BODIED RED WINES

Barbaresco, Barolo, Aglianico, Brunello di Montalcino, Chianti Classico Riserva, Salice Salentino, Taurasi, Vino Nobile di Montepulciano, Cannonau and Primitivo will stand up to roasted vegetables, pastas with slow-cooked, complex meat ragùs, braised meats and game meats. They will also pair with pâté and hard, aged, pungent cheeses. Barolo or Barbaresco and parmesan are a classic combination.

SWEET DESSERT WINES

Malvasia, Moscato d'Asti, Passito, Recioto and Vin Santo are usually served at the end of a meal with cake, chocolate, cookies, tarts and fresh fruit like strawberries, pears and peaches. Vin Santo pairs particularly well with almond biscotti. However, note that the dessert should not be sweeter than the wine you are drinking, or it's likely to dominate.

APERITIVI & DIGESTIVI

Aperitifs and digestifs are incredibly popular in Italy, and the country produces a staggering array of flavoured spirits and herb- and fruit-infused liqueurs. *Aperitivi* are intended to stimulate the appetite before a meal; *digestivi* are meant to settle the stomach and help you to digest your meal.

APERITIVI

Pre-dinner drinks enjoyed with friends over a platter of tasty little snacks, the *aperitivo* is an Italian institution. Some *aperitivi* drinks are virtually unknown outside of Italy, while classics like the Aperol Spritz – Aperol with Prosecco, a splash of soda water and a slice of orange – are famous the world over. Popular *aperitivi*:

APEROL

Bright orange in colour and made to a secret recipe incorporating sweet and bitter oranges, ginseng and various roots, Aperol is the lightest spirit in the world at only 11%. It's usually served over ice, or mixed up into an Aperol Spritz.

CAMPARI

A bitter, bright-red spirit with a palate-cleansing taste, invented in Milan by Gaspare Campari in 1860. The recipe is a secret, but involves an infusion of herbs and fruit. Bitter Campari means the straight drink, while Campari Soda is a pre-mixed bottle of Campari with soda water. Campari is also used in the classic Italian cocktail, the Negroni.

CYNAR

A bittersweet spirit made from 13 herbs and plants, chief among them being artichoke (*cynara scolymus*). Dark brown in colour, it's usually drunk over ice, but can also be mixed with soda water and lemon or orange, or with cola, tonic and bitter-lemon soda. Also popular as a *digestivo*.

GALLIANO

A sweet, bright yellow herbal liqueur created by Livorno brandy producer Arturo Vaccari in 1896. Ingredients include star anise, juniper, musk yarrow, ginger, lavender, peppermint, vanilla and cinnamon. It has a complex, subtle flavour and is used both as a *digestivo* and in cocktails such as the Harvey Wallbanger.

VERMOUTH

The original *aperitivo* spirit, invented in 1786 by Antonio Benedetto Carpano. The name derives from the High German word *werimonta*, a vegetable bitter. This version is wine-based, with added aromatic herbs. There are both red (sweet) and white (dry) versions. Famous brands include Carpano and Cinzano.

DiGESTiVi

Italians love to linger at the table, and *digestivi* provide the perfect excuse. At festive occasions or celebrations, they are an integral part of dessert, which comes in three parts: first the sweet itself, which may be accompanied by a sweet wine or liqueur; then espresso; and finally a *digestivo* like amaro bitters or grappa.

LIQUORI

Sweet alcoholic drinks flavoured with fruits, herbs, spices, flowers, seeds, roots, plants, barks and sometimes even cream, *liquori* get their name from the Latin liqui-facere ('to dissolve'), which refers to the flavours dissolved into the base of each liqueur. *Liquori* aren't typically aged, although they may be rested so that the flavours can marry, and most have an alcohol content of 15–30%. They are made all over Italy and families often have their own *liquori* recipes. The most common are:

ALCHERMES

A red, sweet-spicy liqueur flavoured with cinnamon, cloves, nutmeg and vanilla, popular since the Renaissance when it was favoured by Pope Clemente VII.

AMARETTO

An almost syrupy almond liqueur with a hint of bitterness underneath the sweetness. Used extensively in desserts.

SAMBUCA

Aniseed-flavoured spirit, often poured over a coffee bean in what Italians call *con la mosca* ('with the fly'); the bean is said to bring good luck and isn't usually eaten.

LIMONCELLO

A yellowish-green lemon drink made from fresh Amalfi lemons, pure alcohol, sugar and water. Served ice-cold, it is sweet, fragrant and powerful.

NOCINO

A dark brown *liquori* made from unripe green walnuts, plus coffee beans, vanilla, lemon peel, cloves or allspice.

AMARI

Bitters (*amari*) are the iconic Italian *digestivo*, made by infusing alcohol with a complex variety of herbs and spices. This is done by maceration or distillation, or a combination of the two. The *amaro* is then aged in wooden casks to integrate the flavours, and tends to have a higher alcohol content than most *liquori*. Originally made by monks for medicinal purposes, *amari* is a blanket term for 'bitters' (there are hundreds of different versions in Italy), and many people find them to be an acquired taste. Some of the common *amari* include:

AURUM

Sweetish, brandy-based concoction, flavoured with oranges and with a high alcohol content of 40%. It has roots in ancient Rome.

FERNET

Milan's Fernet Branca is the most popular brand of fernet-style bitters; it's made with 27 rare aromatic herbs and spices from four continents, including saffron, galangal, gentian root and white turmeric.

From top: Grappa
at Jimmi Hut, South
Tyrol; Shots of
limoncello

DISTILLATES

Grappa is Italy's strongest and most popular digestive. With an alcohol content of 30–60%, this fiery, clear distillate is named for the phrase *grappolo d'uva* ('bunch of grapes'), and is made from pomace: the skins, seeds and stems of grapes discarded from the winemaking process. Grappas – of which there are many – can be young (these tend to be harsher) or aged, and some are infused with herbs, fruits or honey. They are usually served ice cold and are excellent paired with chocolate. Grappa originates in the Veneto town of Bassano del Grappa (where you can visit the Poli distillery), but some of the best grappas are made in Friuli by Nonino.

Another strong *digestivo* is Acqua Vita, made by distilling any fruit or vegetable. It could be *mirtilli* (similar to a wild blueberry), *pesche* (peach) or grape varieties such as Chardonnay. The difference is the use of whole fruit rather than the pressings, so the result is a smoother drink.

BAROLO'S AROMATIC WINE

One of Italy's most curious digestivi *is Barolo Chinato, made from Piedmont's famous Barolo wine, which is steeped in aromatic herbs and spices including cardamom seeds, rhubarb, gentian root, coriander, sweet and bitter oranges and China Calissaja bark. Aged for four months in an oak barrel, and then two months in a bottle, it's a smooth and aromatic drink which pairs perfectly with chocolate.*

PHRASES

Right: MAG Cafè,
Milan

Eating Out

Do you speak English (informal/formal/plural)?
Parla/Parli/Parlate inglese?
pahrlah/pahrli/pahrlahte ingleze?

Can you help me, please?
Può aiutarmi, per favore?
pwo ahyootahrmee, per fahvore?

Could you speak a bit more slowly, please?
Potrebbe/Potresti parlare un pò più lentamente, per favore?
potrebbe/potresti parlahre un po pioo lentahmente, per fahvore?

Table for ..., please
Un tavolo per ..., per favore
un tahvolo per ..., per fahvore

Do you have a highchair for the baby?
Ha un seggiolino per la bimba/il bimbo?
ah un sejjoleeno per lah bimbah/il bimbo?

THE MENU

May I see the menu?
Potrei vedere il menù?
potrey vedere il menoo?

Do you have a menu in English?
Avete un menu scritto in inglese?
ahvete un menoo skritto in ingleze?

I'd like the set lunch/tourist menu, please
Vorrei il menù (del giorno/turistico), per favore
vorrey il menoo (del jyorno/tureestiko), per fahvore

What does it include?
Cosa è compreso?
kozah e komprezo?

Does it come with salad?
L'insalata è compresa?
linsahlahtah e komprezah?

ORDERING

I'd like ...   Vorrei ...
vorrey

What is the soup of the day?
Qual è la zuppa/minestra del giorno?
kwahle e lah tsooppah/minestrah del jorno?

Do you have sauce?
Ha della salsa?
ah dellah sahlsah?

Is that dish spicy?
Quel piatto è piccante?
kwel pyahtto e pikkahnte?

Not too spicy please
Non troppo piccante, per favore
non troppo pikkahnte, per fahvore

It's not hot
Non è caldo
non e kahldo

I didn't order this
Non ho ordinato questo
non o ordinahto kwesto

YOU MAY HEAR

Would you like ...?
Vuole **(sg)**/Volete **(pl)** dell'/del ...?
vuole/volete del ...?

Do you want anything to drink?
Cosa vuole **(sg)**/volete **(pl)** da bere?
kozah vuole/volete dah bere?

Enjoy your meal!
Buon appetito!
bwon ahppeteeto

MENU DECODER

meat la carne
lah kahrne

chicken il pollo
il po-lo

poultry il pollame
il pollahme

fish il pesce
il peshe

seafood i frutti di mare
i frootti di mahre

pork il maiale
il mahyahle

cured/processed meats
i salumi/gli insaccati
i sahloomi/ly insahkkahti

JUST TRY IT!

What are they eating?
Cosa stanno mangiando?
kozah stahnno mahnjahndo?

I'll try what she's having
Assaggerò quello che sta
mangiando lei
*ahssahjjero kwello ke stah
mahjahndo ley*

What's the speciality of this region?
Qual è la specialità di questa
regione?
*kwahle e lah spechahleetah di
kwestah rejone?*

What's the speciality here?
Qual è la vostra specialità?
kwahle lah vostrah spechahleeta

What are today's specials?
Quali sono i piatti del giorno?
kwahli sono i pyahtti del jorno?

What can you recommend?
Cosa mi consiglia?
kozah mi konseelyah?

What's that? Cos'è?
koze?

What's in this dish? Quali sono
gli ingredienti in questo piatto?
*kwahli sono ly ingredyentee in
kwesto pyahtto?*

THROUGHOUT
THE MEAL

Please bring me ...?
Mi porta ... per favore?
mi portah ... per fahvore?

> **some water** dell'acqua
> *dellahkwah*
>
> **some wine** del vino
> *del vino*
>
> **some salt** del sale
> *del sahle*
>
> **some pepper** del pepe
> *del pepe*
>
> **some bread** del pane
> *del pahne*

a cup una tazza
unah tahttsah

a fork una forchetta
unah forkettah

a glass un bicchiere
un bikkyere

a knife un coltello
un koltello

a napkin un tovagliolo
un tovahlyolo

a plate un piatto
un pyahtto

a spoon un cucchiaio
un kukkyahyo

a teaspoon un cucchiaino
da tè
un kukkyaheeno dah te

a toothpick uno
stuzzicadenti
uno stuttsikahdentee

SOMETHING WRONG?

This food is ... Questo cibo è ...
kwesto cheebo e

> **cold** freddo
> *freddo*
>
> **stale** stantio/vecchio
> *stahntyo/vekkyo*
>
> **burnt** bruciato
> *broochahto*
>
> **undercooked** poco cotto
> *poko kotto*
>
> **spoiled** avariato
> *ahvahryahto*
>
> **brilliant** eccellente
> *ecchellente*

VEGETARIANS & VEGANS

I'm a vegetarian
Sono vegetariana/o
sono vejetahryahnah/o

I'm a vegan, I don't eat meat or dairy products
Sono vegana/o, non mangio nè carne nè latticini
sono vejetahryahnah/o, non mahnjo ne kahrne ne lahtticheenee

Do you have any vegetarian dishes?
Avete piatti vegetariani?
ahvete pyahtti vejetahryahni?

Does this dish have meat?
C'è carne in questo piatto?
che kahrne in kwesto pyahtto

Does this dish have gelatin?
Questo piatto contiene gelatina?
kwesto pyahtto kontyene jelahteenah?

Can you recommend a vegetarian dish, please?
Ci potrebbe consigliare un piatto vegetariano?
chi potrebbe konsilyahre un pyahtto vejetahryahno?

Could you cook this without meat?
Potreste preparare questo piatto senza carne?
potreste prepahrahre kwesto pyahtto sentsah kahrne?

I don't eat ... Non mangio ...
non mahnjo

I eat only ... Mangio solo ...
mahnjo solo

I prefer to eat ...
Preferisco mangiare ...
preferisko mahnjahre

KOSHER

I'd like a kosher meal
Vorrei un pasto kasher
vorrey un pahsto kahsher

Is this kosher? Questo è kasher?
kwesto e kahsher?

129

INTOLERANCES & ALLERGIES

Is it ...? È ...? *Eee*

> **gluten-free** senza glutine
> *sentsah glootine*
>
> **lactose-free** senza lattosio
> *sentsah lahttozyo*
>
> **wheat-free**
> senza frumento/grano
> *sentsah froomento grahno*
>
> **salt-free** senza sale
> *sentsah sahle*
>
> **sugar-free** senza zucchero
> *sentsah tsukkero*
>
> **yeast-free** senza lievito
> *sentsah lyeveeto*

Does it contain eggs/dairy products?
Contiene uova/latticini?
Kontyene wovah o lahtticheenee?

I'm allergic to ...(peanuts)
Sono allergico a ...(arachidi)
sono ahllerjeeko ah ...(ahrahkeedee)

Is this organic? È biologico?
e byolojeeko?

ORDERING DRINKS

I'd like something to drink Vorrei qualcosa da bere
vorrey kwahlkozah dah bere

Can I have a ... please?
Posso avere una ... per favore?
posso ahvere unah ... per fahvore?

I'd like a glass of ... wine
Vorrei un bicchiere di vino ...
vorrej un bikkyere di vino

> **red** rosso
> *rosso*
>
> **white** bianco
> *byahnko*
>
> **rosé** rosato/rosé
> *rozahto*

CHOOSING WINE

May I see the wine list, please?
Mi fa vedere la lista dei vini, per favore?
mi fah vedere lah leestah dey vini per fahvore?

What is a good year?
Qual è una buona annata?
kwahle unah bwonah ahnnahtah?

May I taste it? Posso degustarlo?
posso degustahrlo?

Which wine would you recommend with this dish?
Quale vino è consigliabile con questo piatto?
kwahle vino e konsilyahbeele kon kwesto pyahtto

Can you recommend a good local wine?
Ci può consigliare un buon vino locale?
chi pwo konsilyahre un bwon vino lokahle?

This wine has a good/bad taste
Questo vino ha un buon/cattivo sapore
kwesto vino ah un bwon kahtteevo sahpore

This wine has a good/bad colour
Questo vino ha un bel/brutto colore
kwesto vino ah un bel/brutto kolore

This wine is corked!
Questo vino sa di tappo!
kwesto vino sah di tahppo

DECODING THE WINE LIST

very dry molto secco
molto sekko

dry secco
sekko

semi-dry/full rotondo
rotondo

fruity amabile
ahmahbeele

Right: Vernazza, in the Cinque Terre; A wine tasting, Castellina in Chianti

lightly sweet dolcigno
dolcheenyo

sweet dolce
dolche

very sweet molto dolce
molto dolche

AT THE END OF THE MEAL

The bill, please
Il conto, per favore
il konto, per fahvore

Is service included in the bill?
Il servizio è compreso nel conto?
il servitsyo e komprezo nel konto?

Let's (not) give her/him a tip
(Non) Diamole/Diamogli la mancia
(non) dyahmole/dyahmoly lah mahnchah

Thank you, that was delicious
Grazie, era squisito/delizioso
grahtsye, erah skweezeeto/delitsyozo

Please pass on our compliments to the chef
Porti per favore i nostri complimenti allo chef
porti per fahvore i nostri komplimentee ahllo chef

At The Bar

Shall we go for a drink?
Andiamo a prendere qualcosa da bere?
ahndyahmo ah prendere kwahlkozah dah bere?

I'll buy you a drink
Ti offro una bevanda
ti offro unah bevahndah

It's on me
Pago io/Offro io
pahgo yo/offro yo

It's my round
Mi occupo io di queste
mi okkupo yo di kweste

You can get the next one
La prossima la paghi tu
lah prossimah lah pahgee too

Okay   D'accordo/Okay/Va bene
dahkkordo/okey/vah bene

What would you like?
Cosa prendi?
kozah prendee?

No ice
Niente ghiaccio/senza ghiaccio
nyente gyahccho/sentsah gyahccho

Can I have ice, please
Posso avere del ghiaccio, per favore?
posso avere del ghyahccho per fahvore?

Same again, please
Facciamo il bis/Un altro, per favore
fahcchahmo il bis; un ahltro per fahvore

Cheers!   Cin cin!
chin chin

I don't drink (alcohol)
Non bevo (alcolici)
non bevo (ahlkoleechee)

This is hitting the spot
Questo è quello che ci vuole!
kwesto e kwello ke vue-oleh

Where is the toilet?
Dove sono i servizi?
dove sono i serveetsee

From top: An espresso; A Turin cafe; Alfreso drinks in Bologna

GETTING ATTENTION AT THE BAR

I'm next!
Dopo tocca a me!/La prossima/Il prossimo/o sono io!
dopo tokkah ah me! lah prossimah/il prossimo/o sono yo!

Excuse me! Scusi!
skoozee

I was here before this lady/ gentleman C'ero prima io di questa/o signora/e!
chero primah yo di kwestah/o sinyorah/e

DRINKS

I'll have ... Prendo ...
prendo

    an anise una sambuca
    unah sahmbookah

    a beer una birra
    unah birrah

    a (bitters/digestive) liqueur
    un amaro/un digestivo
    un ahmahro/uno deegesteevo

    a brandy
    un cognac/un'acquavite
    un konyahk /un ahkwahveete

    a champagne uno champagne/uno spumante
    uno shahmpahn / uno spumahnte

a cocktail un cocktail /un aperitivo
un kokteyl/un ahpereeteevo

a coke una coca
unah kokah

a cider un sidro
un seedro

a grappa una grappa
unah grahppah

a martini un martini
un mahrteeni

a mineral water un'acqua minerale
un ahkwah minerahle

a rum un rum
un room

a whisky un whisky
un wiskee

a glass of wine un bicchiere di vino
un bikkyere di vino

a soft drink un analcolico
un ahnahlkoleeko

Shopping for Food

Where is the nearest (market)?
Dov'è il (mercato) più vicino?
dove il merkahto pyoo vicheeno

When does this shop open?
Quando apre questo negozio?
kwahndo ahpre kwesto negotsyo?

Can I pay by credit card?
Posso pagare con la carta di credito?
posso pahgahre kon lah kahrtah di kredeeto?

Can I taste it?
Lo posso assaggiare?
lo posso ahssahjjahre

Will this keep in the fridge?
Questo si conservà in frigo?
kwesto si konserverah in freego?

Where is (what is) the expiry date?
Dov'è/qual'è la data di scadenza?
dove (kwahle) lah dahtah di skahdentsah?

How much is (a kilo of cheese)?
Quanto costa (un kilogrammo di formaggio)?
kwahnto kostah (un kilograhmmo di formahjjo?)

Do you have anything cheaper?
Ha/Avete qualcosa di meno costoso?
ah/ahvete kwahlkozah di meno kostozo?

Is this the best you have?
Questo è il/la migliore che hai/ha/avete?
kwesto e il/lah milyore ke ahi/ah/ahvete?

What is the local speciality?
Qual'è la specialità locale?
kwahle lah spechahlitah lokahle

BUYING THINGS

How much? Quanto costa?
kwahnto kostah?

Can you give me a discount?
Mi fa lo sconto?
mi fah lo skonto?

Where can I find the (sugar)?
Dove posso trovare il/la/lo/gli (zucchero)?
dove posso trovahre il/lah/lo/ly (tsukkero)?

I am looking for ...
sto cercando ...
sto cherkahndo

Give me (half) a kilo, please.
Me ne dia (mezzo) un kilogrammo per favore
me ne dyah (meddso) un kilograhmmo, per fahvore

I'd like (six slices of ham)
Vorrei (sei fette di prosciutto)
vorrey (sey fette di proshootto)

Can I have a ... Posso avere ...
posso ahvere

a bottle una bottiglia
unah botteelyah

a box una scatola
unah skahtolah

a can
una lattina/un recipiente
unah lahtteenah/ un rechipyente

a packet un pacchetto
un pahkketto

a sachet/bag
una bustina/una borsa
unah busteenah/unah borsah

a tin of ... un barattolo di ...
un bahrahttolo di ...

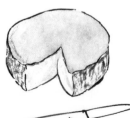

WHAT'S ON THE LIST?

I need ... Mi serve/Mi servono ...
mi serve/mi servono ...

I'd like some
Vorrei del/dei/delle ...
vorrey del/dey/delle ...

biscuits biscotti
biskotti

bread pane
pahne

butter burro
burro

cheese formaggio
formahjjo

chocolate cioccolato
chokkolahto

eggs uova
wovah

flour farina
fahreenah

frozen foods surgelati
surjelahtee

fruit and vegetables
frutta e verdura
froottah e verdoorah

ham prosciutto
proshootto

honey miele
myele

ice-cream gelato
jelahto

jam marmellata/
confettura di frutta
*mahrmellahtah/
konfettoorah di froottah*

margarine margarina
mahrgahreenah

mayonnaise
maionese
mahyoneze

mustard
senape/mostarda
senahpe/mostahrdah

olive/sunflower oil
olio d'oliva/di girasole
*lolyo doleevah/di
jeerahsole*

pepper pepe
pepe

salt sale
sahle

sugar zucchero
tsukkero

vinegar aceto
ahcheto

yoghurt yogurt
yogoort

olives olive
oleeve

black nero
nero

green verde
verde

stuffed ripiena/o
ripyenah/o

Family Meals

You're a great cook!
Sei un cuoco/una cuoca
eccezionale!
*sej un kwoko/unah kwokah
ecchetsjonahle*

This is brilliant!
È eccellente!
e ecchellente

If you ever come to...I'll cook you a local dish
Se verrai/verrete in... ti/vi cucinerò
un piatto locale/tipico
*se verrahj/verrete in...ti/vi
kuchinero un pjahtto lokahle/
tipiko*

Do you have the recipe for this?
Hai la ricetta di questo piatto?
ahj lah richettah di kwesto pjahtto

Is this a family recipe?
Questa è una ricetta di famiglia?
*kwestah e unah richettah
difahmiljah*

The ingredients of this recipe are ...
Gli ingredienti di questa ricetta
sono ...
*lye ingredyentee di kwestah
richettah sono ...*

Are the ingredients local?
Gli ingredienti sono locali?
ly ingredjentee sono lokahli

I've never had a meal like this before
Non ho mai gustato un pasto
simile prima d'ora
*non o mahj gustahto un pjahtto
simile primah dorah*

Could you pass the (salt) please
Puoi passarmi il (sale) per favore?
*pwoj pahssahrmi il (sahle) per
fahvore*

Thanks very much for the meal
Molte grazie per il pasto
molte grahtsje per il pahsto

I really appreciate it
L'ho apprezzato molto
lo ahpprettsahto molto

Clockwise from left:
A family settle down to
lunch al fresco; Pasta
with wild hare; Gelato in
Milan; The historic centre
of Modena

REGIONS

It might look like a boot, but food-obsessed Italy feels more like a decadently stuffed Christmas stocking. One of the world's most revered cuisines, Italian food encompasses a rich cache of regional cooking styles, which together reflect the country's geographic and cultural variety.

Italy is relatively small (less than half the size of Texas), but it is densely populated, highly urbanised and cultured, and has a very long and venerable history. From the fall of the Roman Empire in 476 CE until the country was finally unified in 1870, Italy was made up of independent and highly competitive city-states, which spent much of their time fighting each other and fending off encroaching neighbours and foreign invaders – and thanks to this historic regionalisation, Italy has maintained an extraordinary culinary diversity within its borders.

Today, Italy is made up of 20 regions, each of which has a distinctive geography and climate. In the north, the Alps routinely reach altitudes over 2000m (6562ft) and winters are cold and harsh, whereas semi-arid and tropical conditions prevail in the south. Some regions are landlocked, others seaward facing, and others still are characterised by gentle rolling hills or marshes. As a result, each region's ingredients, food customs, cooking preferences and techniques are highly individualised, and even though many staples (such as pasta, olive oil or tomatoes) are shared, the cooks of each town, valley or village will make a dish in vastly different ways.

So as you explore the country on your gastronomic odyssey, expect culinary surprises at every turn. But wherever you go, you'll find that the common thread throughout Italy is an unbreakable link between food and the locals' sense of identity. From the quality of the produce to the reverence for tradition, eating here is all about passion, pride and *godere la vita* (enjoying life).

PROTECTED DESIGNATION OF ORIGIN

DOP (Protected Designation of Origin) and IGP (Protected Geographical Indication) accreditation is important: there is a huge amount of money at stake. At last count, Italy had 221 DOP and IGP products, and a total of 4698 accredited regional specialities – a number unrivalled by any other European country, and generating annual sales of around €33 billion. In a world where consumers are ever more alert to the quality of produce and anonymous ingredients, the labels that signal an accredited product – red and yellow for DOP, blue and yellow for IGP – are priceless.

VALLE D'AOSTA

Bordered by France, Switzerland and Piedmont, Italy's smallest region is an insular Alpine valley, with a unique larder stocked with marvellous fatty cheeses, barrels of butter and big plates of steaming polenta.

AN ANCIENT CROSSROADS

Safe in the embrace of its saw-toothed mountains, the Valle d'Aosta preserves many ancient culinary traditions. Its principal city, Aosta, has been a hub since the Roman era, when the region got its 'Valley of Augustus' name. The area's dairy products were celebrated even then – Pliny and Strabo praised the rich milk and tangy cheese of the *bos alpinus* (Alpine cattle). Pilgrims, too, relied upon the hospitality of mountain villages to make their way along the Via Francigena to Rome, while monks left behind their knowledge of aromatic herbs and botanicals, which live on in unique distillates such the Génépy herbal liqueur.

The French, who controlled the valley from the 11th century until Italian unification in 1870, added the local love of butter, *boudin* (blood sausage), herb-spiced Jambon de Bosses (cured ham) and cinnamon-flavoured *saouseusse* (sausage). A 15th-century fresco in the Challant family's Castello di Issogne depicts a market scene that includes the first image of the Aosta's famous Fontina cheese, key ingredient of the local take on Swiss fondue. To the north, ancient medieval German and Swiss influences leaked into the Lys Valley, where an isolated German-speaking community called Walsers remain, making *chnolle* polenta dumplings, and *chnéfflene* batter-balls with sour cream and speck.

FONTINA: THE PRIDE OF THE VALLEY

Of all the Valle d'Aosta's food products, Fontina cheese is the most iconic. Made here since the 12th century, and now with protected status, Fontina is used in a huge number of local dishes, most notably *fonduta* (similar to fondue), although you'll also find it layered over polenta, stuffed into veal cutlets (*cotoletta alla valdostana*) and melted into soups. Production of Fontina is strictly controlled: it

POLENTA, NOT PASTA

Unlike much of Italy, the classic carb in the valley isn't pasta, nor even the rice much-loved in neighbouring Piedmont, but polenta, cooked in a copper pot over a wood fire. Polenta is traditionally a food of the poor, made from corn flour and water and served either 'hard' (in spongy slices) or 'soft' (like creamed potato). But here, they mix in rich cheeses such as Fontina, Toma or Maccagno, drizzle in melted butter, and serve it with a glass of medium-bodied Enfer d'Arvier red wine.

Left: Alpine nibbles in the Valle d'Aosta
Right: A dish of polenta with Fontina cheese

can only be made from the whole milk of Valdostane cows, which must be obtained in one milking, and is aged for 80 days. The result is a strong, punchy flavour and a smooth, fatty texture.

The process doesn't end there. The remaining whey can be further heated to 82°C (180°F), when the addition of a little vinegar causes the fat to float to the surface to create *brossa*, a rich, grainy cream traditionally eaten with warm polenta. The rest solidifies to become *seras*, a premium fresh ricotta which, when mixed with garlic, oil, chilli, juniper, fennel and cumin, becomes *salignön*. The latter is usually served as a starter on wafer-thin *miasse*, maize crackers. Other notable cheeses include the semi-sweet Fromadzo, which mixes in goat's milk, juniper and wild cumin; savoury Toma di Gressoney; and mild Reblec, a spongy curd cheese which is topped with sugar and ground cinnamon and eaten as dessert.

FOOD FIT FOR RURAL LIFE

Step into any mountain inn and you'll likely be presented with specialities such as silky Lard d'Arnad; milk and chestnut soup; polenta slices with buttery Toma cheese, or slow-braised, wine-soaked Saint-Oyen ham. This is protein-rich food, designed to ward off the mountain cold and fuel strenuous hikes and hard work. But while Valdostan cuisine is hearty and humble, it doesn't lack sophistication. Having had to rely almost exclusively on what could be grown, reared and produced locally, valley inhabitants have, over the centuries, become expert bee-keepers, mycologists, fruit producers, cheesemakers, smokers and preservers.

Strong, salted, prosciutto-style meats are also central in the diet, most notably *motzetta* (originally made with the goat-like chamois, but now with beef, goat, deer or boar), salted beef and *teuteun*, corned cow udder preserved with sage, rosemary and juniper berries. In autumn, walnuts and chestnuts are gathered to flavour salumi, soups, biscuits and grappa, while rye and wheat harvests produce *pan ner* (black bread), the nutty loaves you find on every table. There isn't much large-scale farming up here, so vegetables don't feature highly, although onions and cabbage form the base of many stews. Instead of greens, look out for the valley's sweet Pippin and Renetta apples, armfuls of mountain berries and aromatic, rust-coloured Martin Sec pears.

Don't Miss

➔ **Fonduta** Melted Fontina cheese with flour, milk and egg yolks, served with rye bread.

➔ **Carbonade Valdostana** Beef stewed with onions, red wine, herbs and juniper berries.

➔ **Seupa à la Vapelenentse** A soup of layered cabbage, leftover bread and Fontina cheese simmered in beef stock.

➔ **Polenta concia** Soft or hard polenta layered with Fontina or Toma cheese, butter and parmesan.

➔ **Tegole** Tuile-like biscuits flavoured with hazelnuts or almonds, vanilla and honey.

➔ **Copa** A hard Christmas rye loaf, traditionally aged in attics for months and served in milk or soup.

THE FRIENDSHIP CUP

If you've ever spent a day skiing and then found yourself holed up in a cosy chalet, you'll know the close camaraderie that mountain life engenders. It is this strong belief in community and loyalty that is behind the caffè alla valdostana, a way of drinking coffee from a shared 'friendship cup'. The ornate wooden 'cup' has multiple spouts from which members of the group sip the citrus- and grappa-infused coffee as they pass it around counterclockwise. All of the coffee must be drunk before the cup is placed back on the table, and as you can't be sure you'll get the same spout each time you take a sip, you need to be confident in your friendship with those you raise the cup with.

PIEDMONT

A large, fertile region whose name translates as 'at the foot of the mountains', Piedmont produces some of Italy's most luxurious gastronomic treats: Barolo wine, white truffles, creamy *gianduja* chocolate and the lean, velvety Piedmontese beef, which many consider to be Italy's answer to Wagyu.

Piedmont is also an original member of Italy's Slow Food movement: it was here that local journalist Carlo Petrini and his group of *neoforchettoni* ('big forks', or foodie) friends dreamed up the Slow Food idea over a good glass of Barolo in Fontanafredda's La Bella Rossa restaurant.

A LUXURIOUS LARDER

Piedmont is Italy's second largest region after Sicily, and its gentle landscape of rolling hills and wide-open pastures produces some of the country's most sophisticated food. Italy's finest cattle are reared here, producing a beef that is leaner, higher in protein and healthier than that of most other breeds. And the vines that cover some 500 sq km (193 sq miles) of land produce some of the country's most celebrated wines,

from Barolo, Barbaresco, Nebbiolo, Dolcetto and Barbera reds to Cortese di Gavi white. The cooking, too, has a sophisticated elegance, influenced by neighbouring France and Switzerland.

Known as the *trifola d'Alba Madonna* (truffle of the White Madonna), the world's finest white truffles (*tuber magnatum*) grow in abundance in the countryside around Alba and Asti, and whether they're shaved over a plate of *tajarin* (the thin egg pasta popular in Piedmont) or a bowl of beef- and cabbage-stuffed ravioli *del plin*, they impart an earthy depth to dishes along with a subtle petrol aroma (in a good way). Truffles also feature heavily in the region's pastas and risottos; the latter is a Piedmontese highlight as Vercelli, set in flood plains at the foot of the

Alps, is the rice capital of Europe. Finally, the world-famous hazelnut chocolate, *gianduja* (or *gianduia*) originated in Turin in 1806, when the city's famous confectioners sought to stretch their cocoa supplies in the face of Napoleon's import bans. The region's abundant hazelnut harvest provided the perfect solution, and thus *gianduja* was born by blending cocoa with a paste of roasted and ground hazelnuts.

PIEDMONT produces SOME OF ITALY'S most luxurious GASTRONOMIC TREATS

From top: Fugascina biscuits in Mergozzo; Rice paddy fields in Novara; Veal with tuna sauce and capers

CAPITAL OF RICE

Most Italian rice (*riso*) is cultivated around the towns of Novara and Vercelli; in fact, Piedmont and neighbouring Lombardy produce the majority of Europe's rice crop, while some 90% of the sushi rice eaten across Europe is also of Piedmontese origin. The region's farmers grow the Arborio and Carnaroli varieties alongside a network of canals that flood the paddies each April, at the beginning of the growing season. Traditionally, the type of rice grown in Italy is known as Japonica, which produces a rounder grain than rice such as basmati. As well as Carnaroli and Arborio, local varieties include the rarer mahogany-coloured Venere and the red Ermes.

Classic Carnaroli and Arborio are perfect for the Piedmontese staple, risotto. Their high starch content ensures that the grains retain their shape while cooking, and slowly release starch into the cooking liquid to create the creamy consistency required of a good risotto. In Piedmont, risotto is usually prepared with a single ingredient – such as local mushrooms, truffles, cheese, seasonal vegetables or local wines like Barolo – to showcase the flavour. To try risottos at their best, book at table at the Michelin-starred Ristorante Christian e Manuel at Hotel Cinzia in Vercelli, where a whole section of the menu is dedicated just to risotto dishes.

PIEDMONTESE BEEF

Piedmont's prized cattle produce some of the world's healthiest red meat, lower in fat and cholesterol even than chicken. They possess a unique gene mutation identified as an 'inactive myostatin allele', which causes what's known as double-muscling and results in meat that has a higher lean-to-fat ratio, less marbling and is extremely tender. The milk produced by the cattle is also top quality, and is used to make Castelmagno, Bra Duro, Raschera and Toma Piemontese cheeses.

Below: Rum-infused
bunet dessert

Don't Miss

➔ **Bagna cauda** A savoury dip made of anchovy, garlic, oil and butter, served warm with raw vegetables for dunking.

➔ **Vitello tonnato** Boiled slices of veal, cooked with herbs and wine, and served cold with a creamy sauce made of tuna, anchovies, eggs and capers.

➔ **Tajarin burro e salvia** A fine *taglierini* pasta, made only with egg yolks and served simply with sage and butter.

➔ **Panissa alla Vercellese** A thick, rich risotto dish made with lard, pork rind, borlotti beans and vegetables.

➔ **Brasato al Barolo** Beef braised for hours in a base of onions, celery, carrots, herbs and Barolo wine, and served on a bed of polenta.

➔ **Bunet** A mousse-like chocolate dessert flavoured with rum, cocoa and amaretti biscuits.

WINE OF KINGS

Arguably Italy's most famous wine, Barolo is produced from the thin-skinned, low-yield Nebbiolo grape, which is high in acid and tannins. It has a minimum ageing requirement of three years, or five years for a riserva; for the very best bottles, you may need to wait up to 20 years for the full flavour to express itself. On the eye, Barolo is a deep-red garnet colour, while flavours associated with it include rose flower, tar, truffles, moist earth, leather and dried herbs. The wine is produced in the 11 comunes of Barolo, southwest of Alba, the most historic of which is Fontanafredda. Pair Barolo with barbecued meat, mushroom risotto, steak, charcuterie, truffles and hard cheeses.

LiGURiA

Surprisingly, given its lack of agricultural land, the Italian Riviera is famous for its food: fat anchovies, fragrant lemons, some of the country's best olives and vibrant-green pesto sauce. Farming is carried out on ingeniously terraced cliff-faces, while impossibly-situated fishing villages serve up seafood delights.

VEGETARIAN HEAVEN

Liguria provides the perfect example of how Italians have adapted to their landscape in order to coax out a delicious array of food from inhospitable surrounds. The challenging mountainous topography offers little room for grazing livestock, so meat-eating is minimal here (save for dishes containing hare), and cheese is largely imported from nearby Lombardy. Instead, the diet offers a startling array of vegetable-based dishes, pastas, breads and an abundance of prime seafood such as rare red prawns, mussels, sea bass and cuttlefish.

Although challenging in one regard, the high mountains create a unique microclimate that supports produce you might think more typical of the south: garlic, citrus, tomatoes, artichokes (Liguria has its own *carciofo spinoso di Albenga* variety), pine nuts and basil all thrive here. Unlike other northern Italian regions, olive oil (rather than lard or butter) forms the base of most dishes, thanks to the DOP-protected *olio di olive della Riviera Ligure*. Wild herbs, too, are a highlight, with dishes enhanced by dandelions, watercress, rosemary, sage and, of course, the region's famous basil. Look out, too, for rarer plants like *pettine di Venere* (a fennel-like herb),

pimpinella (a herb with walnut and anise flavours) and *grespino* (a bitter salad green).

The Ligurian table is characterised by regional pastas such as knobbly *trofie*, covered in basil-rich *pesto alla Genovese* or the creamy *salsa di noci*, a walnut, cheese and cream salsa. Ravioli, too, hail from here and along with the similar *pansotti* are stuffed with wild herbs and greens such as chard and spinach. There are also *torta verde*, vegetable pies filled with artichokes, courgettes, spinach and chard, and encased in a thin pastry made with olive oil rather than butter. At Easter, the iconic *torta Pasqualina* is enriched with eggs and ricotta and wrapped in a flaky pastry made of 33 layers of dough, representing the years of Christ's life.

FOCACCIA & FARINATA FLATBREADS

You can now find focaccia all over Italy, but *focaccia Genovese* – fairly thin and flavoured with salt, olive oil and sometimes rosemary – is the original. But, spend a week

along the Italian Riviera and you'll quickly learn that there are dozens of focaccias.

To the east of Genoa, the *galletta di Camogli* is a crisp focaccia more akin to a biscuit that was supposedly invented for the town's sailors to take on long voyages. In nearby Recco, the delicious focaccia spreads mild creamy cheese (usually Stracchino or Crescenza) between two thin slices of bread made without yeast; the roots of this moreish treat can be traced back to the Saracen invasions of the early Middle Ages. San Remo, on the Riviera di Ponente, has concocted *sardenaira*, a pizza-like focaccia topped with tomatoes, onions, capers and – as the name implies – sardines. And, yes, you've seen right: Ligurians think nothing of dipping a slice of focaccia into their morning coffee.

Second only to focaccia is the chickpea flatbread *farinata*, made from a mixture of chickpea flour, olive oil and water and baked into a thin, savoury flatbread. In Liguria it is quickly fried to leave the centre soft, and the taste is slightly sweet and creamy. It may have been influenced by nearby Provence (Nice has a similar flatbread called *socca*), or the influence may run the other way, so Ligurians think. Other versions of it are Tuscany's *cecina* and Sicily's *panelle*.

PESTO GENOVESE

Liguria's biggest gift to the world is undoubtedly Genoa's famous sauce of pounded basil leaves, pine nuts, olive oil, parmesan (or pecorino) and garlic. But the pesto you'll taste here is superior to anything you'll sample elsewhere due to the deep-green, DOP-protected basil used to make it. Genovese basil is sweet and full of flavour and the very best comes from Prà, a district to the west of the city. Pesto is actually a generic term for anything made by pounding with a pestle, so you can find other versions made with fava or broad beans or pistachios.

TAGGIASCA OLIVES

Although olives typically thrive in the hotter climate of the south, Liguria's Taggiasca olives are some of the best in the country. They grow on Cailletier trees (better known in France as Niçoise), which cling to steep, sea-facing cliffs fanned by the balmy Tramuntana breeze. The tiny, succulent olives are both eaten and pressed to form one of the best virgin olive oils in Italy. Because the olives have a low acid content, the oil tastes sweet with a hint of fresh almonds and hazelnut; it's a key ingredient of *pesto alla Genovese* as well as Niçoise salad.

Clockwise from left:
Crushing a pesto
sauce; Walking the
Sentiero Azzurro;
Food served at
Frantoio Sant'Agata
d'Oneglia oil mill

Don't Miss

➔ **Pissalandrea** A savoury
flatbread made of leavened dough
topped with tomato and onion
sauce, salted anchovies, oregano
and Taggiasca olives.

➔ **Pasta alla Genovese** Trofie
pasta, boiled potatoes and beans
coated in handmade local pesto.

➔ **Focaccia di Recco** Simply
the best cheese sandwich ever,
made from layering stracchino
cheese between two layers of crispy
flatbread.

➔ **Pansotti** Triangular ravioli
filled with a mixture of wild
herbs, greens and cheese, and
covered in *salsa di noci* (cheesy
walnut sauce).

➔ **Condiglione** The Ligurian
version of salad Niçoise, featuring
onion, tomato, pepper, anchovy,
olives, garlic, boiled egg, tuna and
olive oil.

➔ **Castagnaccio** A gluten-free,
chestnut-flour cake filled with
pine nuts and raisins, combined
with olive oil and topped with
orange zest or honey.

Left: Winding streets down to Lake Como

LOMBARDY

Italy's richest region, Lombardy covers four distinct culinary zones: the Po Valley has rice paddies and rivers frequented by game birds; the glittering glacial lakes teem with freshwater fish; cows and goats graze Alpine foothills producing milk and cheese; and the mountains are covered with chestnut forests.

MARVELLOUS MILAN

De Magnalibus Mediolani (The Marvels of Medieval Milan) was written in 1288 by Milanese monk Bonvesin de la Riva. In his depiction of his home town, Bonvesin gives an insight into the surprisingly rich diet of one of Europe's largest medieval cities. Butchers, fishmongers and bakers were important

men in Milan, members of powerful guilds, and it's no wonder when you consider the animals, wild birds, poultry, fruits and fish they supplied. Dishes such as *nervetti* (veal cartilage), *busecca* (tripe stew), *bollito* (boiled meats) and *carpione* (fried, floured fish) were already standard; Bonvesin also lists damascene plums (damsons), early figs, hyssop and white horehound – exotic ingredients even by today's standards. And even back then, landlocked Milan was one of the best places in Italy to eat fish, thanks to its access to the

northern lakes and the supply of fresh prawns from the city's moat.

Today, Milan is Italy's wealthiest city, and its dining scene incorporates some of the country's brightest Michelin-starred kitchens (Ristorante Berton, Seta, Cracco and Alice) alongside traditional regional trattorias and an increasingly interesting ethnic food scene. Local favourites include *cotoletta* (breadcrumbed veal) and mellow, yellow risotto. Other gold standards are osso buco, a veal-shank stew

scattered with spritzy parsley, garlic and lemon-rind *gremolata*; stuffed courgette (zucchini) flowers; the golden polenta that accompanies meat or mushroom dishes; and panettone, the brioche-like Christmas bread. Fish, too, remains a staple – the city hosts the largest wholesale fish market in Europe.

REGIONAL VARIATIONS

Beyond Milan, the food of this region varies between hearty meat-and-cheese mountain cooking and the lighter cuisine of the Italian lakes and lowland floodplains, where fish and vegetables feature more prominently.

In the Alpine foothills, the cooking of Brescia and Bergamo features strong flavours. In

Left: Risotto alla Milanese with saffron
Right: Dining al fresco

Bergamo, polenta is served 'wet' with almost everything, including dishes such as *schisöl* (polenta cooked with cheese and mushrooms) and the *polenta e osei* (sweet polenta cake garnished with chocolate birds). Alpine herds provide an ample supply of meat for braised stews (*brasato*), *casoncelli* (ravioli stuffed with sausage meat) and Brescia's famous *pestöm* (minced pork salami), as well as milk for famous cheeses such as Grana Padano, Bagòss and Rosa Camuna. Further north in the Valtellina valley, you'll find Bitto cheese, *bresaola* (air-cured beef) and buckwheat pasta.

The glacial lakes of Maggiore, Como and Garda, on the other hand, are fish-focused. Perch, pike, tench, shad, sardines, local *lavarello* (whitefish) and eels are all plentiful, served lightly fried, grilled or poached. More elaborate treatments include fish soups, marinades and risottos. The surrounding mountain valleys offer up Taleggio and Formagella cheeses along with cured meats. The sunny shores of Lake Garda yield excellent lemons, fruity olive oils and wine, while Maggiore is famous for its Gorgonzola cheeses, as well as chestnuts, rhododendron-flavoured honeys and cured goat's leg from the Vigezzo Valley. To the south, around Novara, farms cultivate innumerable rice varieties, including the rare Black Venus.

Finally, in the fertile River Po Valley, vegetable gardens, orchards, rice and maize fields stretch between the prosperous patrician towns of Pavia, Lodi, Cremona and Mantua. This was traditionally a land of peasant farmers, and fruits, vegetables and polenta loom large on menus alongside river fish, frogs, poultry, wild boar, horse, salami and game birds. The rich Renaissance city of Mantua, meanwhile, is addicted to *tortelli alla zucca* (spiced pumpkin pasta).

LIVING WELL IN DIFFICULT TIMES

A Jewish intellectual working in Fascist Milan, Fernanda Momigliano was also a cookery writer – her first book, Vivere bene in tempi difficili *(Living Well in Difficult Times) showed Italian women how they might enjoy good food on diminishing budgets following the 1929 Wall Street Crash. Her follow-up book,* Eating Italian *(1936), includes 16 Jewish recipes typical of Lombardy. They range from carp and porcini mushrooms cooked in white wine to a saffron risotto prepared on the eve of the Sabbath, as well as goose salami, a specialist product from Mortara that now holds the prestigious Slow Food badge of approval.*

Don't Miss

● **Risotto alla Milanese** Milan's most famous dish, enriched with bone marrow and butter and enhanced with saffron and parmesan.

● **Cotoletta alla Milanese** A flattened veal cutlet, drenched in egg and breadcrumbs then fried in butter. Very similar to the German schnitzel.

● **Casoncelli** A stuffed pasta filled with meat, breadcrumbs, parmesan, nutmeg and a reduced broth.

● **Lavarello con salsa verde** A typical dish from Lake Como: whitefish marinated in a parsley and garlic sauce.

● **Risotto alla Certosina** Risotto dish invented by monks containing crayfish, frogs and freshwater perch.

● **Pizzoccheri alla Valtellinese** Strips of flat buckwheat pasta in a cabbage, potato and grana padano cheese sauce.

FOREIGN INFLUENCES

Milan's generations of internal Italian immigrants have injected the cuisine of virtually every region into the lifeblood of the city, where you'll often find Genovese, Piedmontese and Tuscan dishes sharing menu space with local Lombardy classics. Milan's increasingly diverse global population has also influenced the city's eating scene. Unusually for Italy, Japanese and Chinese restaurants are commonplace here and the cuisines of India, the Middle East, sub-Saharan Africa and, most recently, Latin America are all increasingly represented. The best of them include Michelin-starred Japanese restaurant Tokuyoshi, cult eatery Casa Ramen Super, top-drawer Dim Sum and gourmet kebab shop NÚN.

Left: The towering
Dolomites behind
the village of Santa
Maddalena

TRENTINO—ALTO ADIGE

Dominated by the sawtoothed Dolomites, the semi-autonomous provinces of Trentino–Alto Adige are a fascinating melange of Italian and Germanic culture. Nowhere is this more evident than on the plate, where you'll find unique dishes like *knödel* (dumplings), *casunziei* (beetroot-filled pasta with poppy seeds) and *apfelküchel* (apple cake).

MOUNTAIN CULTURE

Alpine influences in Trentino-Alto Adige, which is also known as Trentino-South Tyrol, signify the region's continuing close relationship with its Austrian and Swiss neighbours. Many residents speak German or the ancient Ladin language, and the food reflects this hybrid character, too, with distinct dishes such as *spätzle* (a Germanic fresh-egg pasta), *canederli* (bread dumplings), *fortaies* (thick fried pancakes) and *schuttelbröt* (a thin, crisp bread).

With plenty of top-quality grazing land, meat is a big feature on menus. Beef and lamb appear in hearty stews or served on a bed of polenta, while game is eaten throughout the year, usually served with a berry or apple sauce.

Sausages (with sauerkraut) are also popular, and there are dozens of cured meat products, most famous among them being speck. The latter is one of Italy's most famous salumi, a deep-flavoured ham cured with bay and juniper and then smoked and aged. It's typically served with dark rye bread and spectacular mountain cheeses such as Stilfser and Vinschger.

The mountains, too, influence this unusual cuisine, as they are home to a unique ecosystem. A healthy mountain meadow can contain over a hundred different plant species, many of which are foraged for the kitchens of the region's extraordinary number of Michelin-starred restaurants. There are some fifty edible wild herbs here, including the likes of lady's mantle (a mild, bitter green herb used to flavour bread and soups), silver birch (the ground leaves are used as seasoning), wood sorrel (whose sharp-tasting leaves are featured in salads) and Icelandic moss, a lichen used in bread, porridge and soup.

MOUNTAIN MICHELIN STARS

Restaurants in Trentino-Alto Adige hold a staggering collection of 25 Michelin stars — and Alta Badia is home to some of the best restaurants, including Norbert Niederkofler's world-famous St Hubertus restaurant. In March, Alta Badia also hosts the annual gastronomic Care's Ethical Chef Festival and the Wine Skisafari; from July to September organic farmers markets take over the region's village squares.

PASTA AND DUMPLINGS

Pasta isn't the principle starch in Trentino-Alto Adige, although you will find tagliatelle served with game-meat ragù, and small, half-moon *schlutzkrapfen* ravioli filled with spinach and ricotta. Pasta here is often made with different types of flour such as kamut, farro or spelt; *turtres*, for example, is made from a mixture of rye and wheat.

More popular than pasta are dumplings. Chief among these are *canederli*, cheesy bread and speck dumplings served with a rich beef broth. There's also the homicidally named *strangola-preti* ('priest stranglers'), gnocchi stuffed with spinach and cheese. Most unique of all, however, are *spätzle*, created by pushing an egg pasta dough through a colander into boiling water. They are usually served in soups or with beef or cream sauces. *Zuppa d'orzo* (barley soup) is also a Tyrolean staple, a simple mountain soup packed with pearl barley, beans, vegetables, milk and smoked pork.

CHEESE, GLORIOUS CHEESE

Home to some of the richest pastures in the world, Trentino-Alto Adige is known for its wonderful cheeses, which number among Italy's best. There are over 200 local varieties, often made in small mountain farms where free-ranging cows and sheep graze in high-altitude wildflower meadows; the rich and flavourful milk that they produce is usually processed into cheese within 24 hours. Some of the finest regional cheeses include:

Stilfser (Stelvio) A centuries old, DOP-protected cheese made from brined cow's milk. It has a semi-soft, elastic texture and a strong, spicy flavour.

Vinschger A semi-hard Alpine cheese punctuated by tiny holes. Made from milk produced by cows in the Vinschgau Valley, it is smooth and fruity with a slight spice finish.

Alta Badia A hard cow's cheese not dissimilar to Gruyere, but with a more complex, nutty, milkier flavour. It's aged for 180 days and the flavours develop with time.

Luis Trenker A unique, mature Tyrolean cheese with a black rind and a creamy texture. On the palate you'll detect flavours of honey, caramel, fruit and chocolate that linger in the mouth.

Lagrein Named after the regional wine in which it's washed, which has been infused with added herbs, spices and garlic, this cheese has a creamy, spicy flavour and pairs perfectly with a glass of Lagrein wine.

Gran Capra A crumbly, grainy, sweetish goat's cheese with a fragrant aroma and the flavour of a flowery mountain meadow. It is ripened for nine months.

Hay-milk mozzarella The Tyrol's unique take on Italy's most famous soft cheese, made from the milk of cows with a heavy hay diet. The result is rich, mild, milky-sweet flavour.

Graukäse The unappealingly named 'grey cheese' was traditionally a poor man's staple, made with milk from which the fat had been removed for butter. It contains around 0.5% fat, and is acid-cured which gives it a sour flavour and pungent aroma.

MOUNTAIN WINES

Like the cuisine, the wines of Trentino-Alto Adige are unique and surprising, and the vast majority of them have a DOC classification. Vines love the cool mountain temperatures and sunny hillsides, and produce predominantly crisp white wines with excellent minerality. Indigenous grape varieties include Schiava, Lagrein, Teroldego and Gewürztraminer along with Chardonnay and Pinot Bianco. The former three are red grape varieties, while Gewürztraminer produces white wines. Around the regional capital, Trento, vineyards such as Ferrari and Moser produce very good Italian champagnes using the metodo classico.

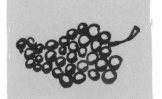

Above: Knödel dumplings

Don't Miss

➲ **Speck** A smoked prosciutto made from pork shoulder, leg and belly, flavoured with spices and juniper.

➲ **Canederli** A dumpling made from stale bread and flavoured with cheese and speck, usually served in a meat broth.

➲ **Strangolapreti** A large bread dumpling filled with spinach and cheese and doused in a brown-butter sauce.

➲ **Spätzle** Tiny, handmade egg noodles typically served with creamy sauces flavoured with speck.

➲ **Tyrolean goulash** A beef stew which, similar to the Hungarian dish, is spiced with paprika and cumin. It's usually served with polenta.

➲ **Kaiserschmarrn** A sweet cara-melised pancake filled with apples, nuts, plums and raisins, dusted with sugar and served with jam.

FRIULI VENEZIA GIULIA

With its triple-barrelled moniker, Friuli Venezia Giulia's multifaceted nature should come as no surprise. Cultural complexity is cherished in this tiny region, tucked away on the borders with Austria and Slovenia, which only became Italian in 1954.

Its landscapes offer profound contrasts, too: an Austrian-influenced cuisine dominates in the perpetually snowy Giulie and Carnic Alps to the north, while grapevines cover the plains of idyllic Il Collio in the centre, and the marshy lagoons of the coast yield fishy delicacies similar to those in Venice, such as mantis shrimps, sea bream, eels and mullet.

A BORDERLAND CUISINE

Slavic, Austrian and Italian influences can all be found in the region's kitchens. There's goulash served with polenta; San Daniele ham, which rivals that of Parma; smoked trout from the Isonzo and Tagliamento rivers; gnocchi made with cherries and prunes; and little *salamini Italiani alla cacciatora*, originally made for hunters and later for the endless streams of soldiers who were stationed on these borders. The bakeries of the regional capital, Trieste, are a scented, sweet delight, while the elegant Austrian-style cafes here specialise in apple strudel and a string of buffet places dole out the city's signature dish, *jota*, a thick soup made with sauerkraut, beans, potatoes and bacon. This is not Italy as we know it.

Further north, climbing into the Carnic and Giulie Alps, *bollito* (boiled-meat stews), *boreto* (Grado's lagoon-fish stew) and *fritto misto* (platters of fried fish) give way to smoked ham products like Speck di Sauris and *muset*, a pork sausage spiced with cinnamon, pepper, coriander and cloves. *Canederli* (dumplings) replace polenta, and venison, chamois, woodcock, mushrooms and mountain cheeses like Montasio and Formadi Frant (a 'crushed' cheese made from mixing offcuts of other cheeses) abound on the dining room tables of traditional *stube* (chalet restaurants).

SAN DANIELE: THE OTHER HAM

There are two world-revered prosciuttos manufactured in Italy: the lean, deliciously nutty (and world famous) ham from Parma, and the dark, exquisitely sweet Prosciutto di San Daniele. It might come as a surprise to find that the latter – Friuli Venezia Giulia's greatest culinary gift to the world – comes from a village of just 8000 people, where it is salted and cured in only 27 *prosciuttifici* (ham-curing plants), each of which is safeguarded by EU regulations.

Standards are strict. San Daniele's prosciutto is made only from the thighs of pigs raised in a

small number of northern Italian regions. Salt is the only method of preservation allowed – no freezing, chemicals or other preservatives can be used. The X factor is, of course, terroir, the land itself. Some *prosciuttifici* claim it's the cool, resinous alpine air meeting the Adriatic's humid, brackish breezes that define their product; others argue that it's about San Daniele's fast-draining soil – such effective ventilation makes for perfect curing conditions.

In late June, the town holds the Aria di San Daniele, a multiday annual ham festival when *prosciuttifici* do mass open-house tours and tastings and there's much gourmet celebrating. San Daniele's tourist office has a list of *prosciuttifici* that also welcome visitors year-round; call ahead to book your tasting.

IL COLLIO

Equidistant from the Austrian Alps and the Adriatic Sea, the gentle, hilly landscape of the Collio has a sunny, breezy microclimate that conspires with the marlstone soil to produce grapes of astonishing fragrance, which yield some of Italy's finest DOC-accredited white wines. The sharp temperature differential between day and night generates layers of complexity and depth of aroma, while the marl and sandstone soil, known locally as *ponca*, imparts salinity and minerality.

Although internationally known varieties such as Pinot Grigio thrive in the area, the star of the show here is the indigenous Friulano grape, which produces full-bodied, aromatic whites with the flavour of apple, pear and almond. Ribolla Gialla is another fabulous grape, creating deep-yellow wines tasting of stone-fruit and citrus. Finally, Malvasia, a popular grape in nearby Slovenia and Croatia, yields wines that are crisp and rich, tasting of pear, golden apples and yellow peaches.

BUFFET, TRIESTE–STYLE

You'll be sure to eat well at a Triestine buffet, but banish any thought of all-you-can-eat meal deals. These rowdy bar-restaurants are a legacy of the city's Austro-Hungarian past; if Trieste's bakeries conjure up Vienna, its buffets are Budapest all over. Usually all-day, all-night affairs, they serve small snacks – cod or courgette (zucchini) fritters, topped toasts and panini – from early morning, which are gobbled up over lunch or at aperitivo time. But come evening, who's here for courgettes? Beef brisket may be a stalwart, but pork – baked, boiled, cured, stuffed into a sausage or fried – is the star attraction. Fresh grated kren (horseradish), capuzi (sauerkraut) and patate in tecia (mashed potatoes, fried up with bacon and caramelised onion) are traditional accompaniments.

Don't Miss

→ **Prosciutto di San Daniele** Friuli's exquisitely sweet, hand cured DOP-protected ham. To be eaten as is, without olive oil.

→ **Jota** A warming winter bean soup with pancetta and potatoes – plus sauerkraut..

→ **Gnocchi alla prugna** Gnocchi made with mashed potato, butter, sugar, cinnamon, prunes and parmesan cheese.

→ **Boreto alla Graisana** A traditional fisherman's stew from Grado, made with the leftover catch of the day cooked in garlic, oil and white wine vinegar, and served with polenta.

→ **Frico** A kind of flat cake, similar to a Swiss rösti, made with potato, onion and Montasio cheese.

→ **Presnitz** A spiral-shaped puff-pastry case stuffed with a variety of nuts, Marsala- and rum-soaked raisins, chocolate and pine nuts.

OSMIZE: POP-UP WINE CELLARS

Osmize (or osmice) predate the pop-up phenomenon by a few centuries, care of an 18th-century Austrian law that gave farmers the right to sell their surplus once a year (the term osmiza comes from the Slovenian word for 'eight', the number of days of the original licence). Today's osmize are mainly held by vineyards on the Carso plateau, which wraps around Trieste, and farm cheeses and cured meats are always on offer. Finding an osmiza is part of the fun: look first for the red arrows, and then for signposts or gates bearing a frasca – a leafy branch hung upside down; you then follow the leafy frasca trail. On arrival, make sure to try the Carso's native wines: white Vitovska and berry-scented Teran.

From left: Hearty jota soup; Testing the temperature of smoking hams

VENETO

The Veneto is one of Italy's most geographically varied regions. It starts high in the mountainous Dolomites and descends down sunny hillsides to the fertile plains of the River Po and on to the Venetian lagoon — and the cuisine here is as happily varied as the landscape.

FROM MOUNTAINS TO THE SEA

The Veneto is made up of seven provinces, some of which are mountainous, some lakeside, some riverine and some beside the sea. This results in a diverse pantry in which meat, fish, grains, produce and dairy are all treated with similar respect. Broadly-speaking, common staples include polenta and risotto, buckwheat *bigoli* spaghetti, a range of regional cheeses, a love of rich meat stews based on beef, duck or horse and, of course, fish from enormous Lake Garda and the Venetian lagoon.

Since the introduction of maize from America, polenta is now mostly made from white biancoperla maize and is served as a side for meat and game dishes. Risotto, meanwhile, is the preferred *primo* (first course), coming from the rice paddies near the river Tartaro, which produce the IGP-protected *vialone nano Veronese* variety. Treviso's famous radicchio is often served as the main ingredient of a standout winter risotto, as is the sweet white asparagus from Bassano del Grappa.

Alongside Lombardy, the Veneto also produces many of Italy's most famous DOP-protected cheeses, including Grana Padano, buttery Asiago and Taleggio, Schiz, Casatella Trevigiana, Montasio, Monte Veronese and Provolone Valpandana. And pretty much everywhere, you'll find Italy's most famous dessert tiramisu, which, according to legend, was created in Treviso by chef Roberto Linguanotto as a 'pick me up' (the loose translation of its name), hence the inclusion of coffee.

FROM THE MOUNTAINS

Alpine Belluno borders Austria, and is where you'll find plates of *capriolo* (roe-deer venison), and semi-hard Schiz cheese served

PADUA'S ANCIENT MARKET

Every day for the past 800 years, Paduans have done their shopping in the huge outdoor markets in Piazza delle Erbe (Herb Piazza) and neighbouring Piazza della Frutta (Fruit Piazza), which together comprise one of the largest markets in Italy and still operate much as they did in the Middle Ages. Dividing the two is the Gothic Palazzo della Ragione, whose arcades hold specialist butchers, cheesemakers, fishmongers and salumerie.

pan-fried on polenta or mushrooms. Also notable is the local *casunziei*, half-moon ravioli from the ski resort of Cortina d'Ampezzo; and *pastin* sausage, made from minced beef and pork and flavoured with white wine and spices.

FROM THE FOOTHILLS OF THE ALPS

Vicenza province spreads across the lower foothills of the Alps, and its notable products are a reflection of its location. Nutty, salty Asiago cheese has been produced on the Asiago plateau for centuries; it's served fresh in sandwiches or aged and crumbled into salads, soups and pastas. Succulent white asparagus from Bassano del Grappa is another wildly popular speciality, picked before the shoots break ground. Bassano is also the source of Italy's most famous grappa, produced using grapes left over from the winemaking process.

FROM THE LAKE SHORE

Verona province marks the western edge of the Veneto and is separated from Lombardy by Lake Garda. Italy's largest lake, Garda has a sunny, Mediterranean microclimate, and the hills on its eastern shore are perfect for winemaking, producing one of Italy's most famous

white wines, Soave, as well as reds such as Amarone, Valpolicella and Bardolino. Amarone, made from partially dried grapes, finds its way into risotto and all sorts of other dishes, while the ancient *pastissada de caval* (horsemeat stew) is enriched with Valpolicella and spices. Verona is also known for *pandoro*, a golden brioche bread similar to Milan's panettone.

FROM THE PLAINS

The area around Treviso is one of Italy's most fertile and is famous for its vegetables, particularly *radicchio rosso di Treviso Tradivo*, an IGP-protected chicory with a mildly bitter taste. Other excellent veg grown here include radicchios from Chioggia and Castelfranco and the celery-like cardoons, as well as peas, beans and artichokes, while the vast fields around Padua are planted with the white biancoperla maize used to make polenta.

Also originating in the Po Valley is Grana Padano, a hard, crumbly cow's cheese that rivals parmesan; and Provolone Valpadana, a sweet, yellow cow's cheese that pairs well with regional wines and is sometimes eaten breaded and fried. Aged, pork-based *sopressa* is the local salumi, and guinea fowl and game birds feature on menus in abundance;

the Paduan hen, *gallina padovana*, is one of the oldest breeds of chicken in Europe. Goose, too, is popular here (a legacy of northern Italy's Jewish community), featuring in *oca in onto padovana*, where the goose meat is salted, marinated in herbs and aged in a process not dissimilar to French confit.

VENETO WINES

The Veneto has been cultivating vines since Etruscan times. On the white front, there is the light, bright, sparkling Prosecco, made using Glera grapes from Conegliano Valdobbiadene; and the fresh, food-friendly, Garganega-based Soave. There are also some serious reds: velvety Valpolicella and big, bold Amarone, made using partially dried grapes from a blend of ancient varieties such as Corvina, Corvinone and Rondinella.

The less well-known Colli Euganei, an orange-scented dessert wine made from Muscat grapes which grow on the volcanic slopes of the Colli Euganei, while Padua can lay claim to Aperol; invented here in 1919, it's typically mixed with prosecco to form the ubiquitous Aperol spritz. Unsurprisingly, Italy's most important wine exhibition, Vinitaly, has been held in Verona since 1967.

Above: Warming risotto al radicchio

Don't Miss

→ **Bigoli con anantra** Buckwheat spaghetti with a duck ragù enriched with wine, rosemary and juniper berries.

→ **Risotto al radicchio** A delicious winter risotto made with sweet onions, red wine and radicchio from Treviso.

→ **Casunziei** Half-moon shaped ravioli, traditionally stuffed with beetroot and poppy seeds although other variations can be found.

→ **Brasato all'Amarone** A stew of beef or veal slowly braised with herbs and red wine (typically Amarone), and served with polenta.

→ **Baccalà alla Vicentina** Vicenza's take on salt cod, cooked here with onions, olive oil, sardines, milk, cheese and parsley, and served on polenta.

→ **Tiramisu** Treviso's famous layered dessert: sweet egg and mascarpone cream over coffee- and Marsala-soaked *savoiardi* biscuits, dusted on top with cocoa powder.

PROSECCO LOWDOWN

The Veneto is home to the worldwide phenomenon called Prosecco, a sparkling wine with a long history. The Romans knew it as 'Pucino', but today, Prosecco comes from sunny hillsides just north of the Piave river between the towns of Valdobbiadene, Conegliano and Vittorio Veneto. You can spot a good Prosecco by its straw-like yellow colouring, which is touched with a tinge of green, and its bubbles should be tiny, numerous and long-lasting in your glass. On the nose, it is fragrant with the scent of white fruits and freshly mown grass, while in the mouth it's crisp and aromatic. These characteristics are not long lasting, so drink Prosecco young when it's full of fizz.

VENICE

Venetian food is not like Italian food, or even that of the Veneto region it sits in. There are far fewer pasta dishes than anywhere else in Italy, but thanks to the city's garden islands and a lagoon's worth of seafood, Venice does promise many local specialities that never make it to the mainland.

THE LAGOON LARDER

Venetian cuisine revolves around the day's catch from the lagoon and the Adriatic Sea. A morning trip to the Rialto, Venice's centuries-old fish market, will get you acquainted with everything from *sardele* (sardines), *sgombro* (mackerel), *gò* (lagoon goby), *folpetti* (baby octopus), *peoci* (mussels) and *seppie* (squid) to seasonal *moeche* (soft-shelled crabs). Fish are usually served whole, with the head and tail on, and the taste is not masked by sauces.

According to Venetian purists, nothing (including lemon) should overpower the fish's characteristic flavour.

It's thanks to this marine life that the lagoon larder is also rich in aquatic birds, which constitute another traditional foodstuff. The meat of other animals, on the other hand, has never been that important – unsurprising when you consider the logistics of transporting and maintaining livestock here. That said, offal is occasionally eaten, including tripe, black pudding, veal cartilage and the famous *luganeghe* sausage.

Vegetarians should rejoice, as side-dishes of Veneto vegetables often steal the show – early risers will notice Venetians risking faceplants in canals to grab *violetti di Sant'Erasmo* (baby purple artichokes), *radicchio Trevisano* (ruffled, red bitter chicory) and Bassano del Grappa's prized white asparagus from produce-laden barges. Polenta also dominates: it's served fried, grilled, crunchy or creamy, and takes the place of rice, potatoes or bread.

VENETIAN FUSION

During the 13th century, Venice spawned a global network of merchants (including Marco Polo) who dominated the lucrative global trade in sugar, spice, coffee, grain and codfish. Venetian cookbooks from that era include recipes for fish with galangal, saffron and ginger, and many of today's classic Venetian dishes, such as sarde in saor (sardines marinated in a tangy onion marmalade), taste vaguely Turkish or Greek, reflecting spice-route flavours. The city's fusion fare can be sampled at places such as Zanze XVI, Bistrot de Venice, Anice Stellato and Osteria Trefanti.

GIRO D'OMBRA

An authentic Venetian giro d'ombra (pub crawl) begins around the Pescaria market by 9am, drinking Prosecco with the fisherfolk toasting a hard day's work that began at 3am. For layabouts, Venice offers a second-chance giro (with cicheti) around noon, visiting the bacari that ring the Rialto Market. Afterwards, it's a long four-hour dry spell until the next giro d'ombra begins in buzzing spots around Campo Santa Margherita in Dorsoduro, Fondamenta dei Ormesini in Cannaregio, Campo Santa Maria Formosa and Via Garibaldi in Castello, and the warren of calli (lanes) around Campo San Bartolomeo and Campo Manin in San Marco.

THE TRADITION OF BACARI

One of the world's oldest republics, Venice invented the democratic tradition of the *bacaro* (bar), where drinks were served alongside *cicheti* (small bites similar to tapas) and a working-class clientele could graze affordably on tasty food. Often standing-room-only, *bacari* are still popular today. Most Venetians begin their evenings by meeting friends over a glass of good wine and something delicious at their local *bacaro*. When it gets too crowded, they skip over the bridges to the next *bacaro* and the next plate of food.

Cicheti range from basic snacks (spicy meatballs, bruschetta with tomato and basil) to highly inventive small plates: think white Bassano asparagus and plump lagoon shrimp wrapped in pancetta; Fassone beef and peppers; creamy cheeses from Monte Veronese; wild boar salami; mixed plates of garden greens and steamed mussels; or fragrant, bite-sized bread rolls crammed with tuna, chicory and horseradish. To accompany, request *qualcosa di particolare* (something interesting) and your sommelier will accept the challenge to reach behind the bar for an unusual Veneto varietal. Even ordinary grapes take on extraordinary characteristics in growing areas that range from marshy to mountainous. Speciality bars like Vino Vero, Estro, Malvasia all'Adriatico Mar, Salvmeria, Ossi di Seppia, Al Prosecco, El Sbarlefo and La Cantina uphold Venice's time-honoured tradition of selling good stuff by the glass.

Clockwise from left:
Aperol Spritz and
cicchetti; A food stall
at the Rialto market;
The preparation of
Baccalà mantecato

Don't Miss

➔ **Baccalà mantecato** Salt cod
cooked in milk then whisked with
olive oil until soft, and served on
grilled white polenta.

➔ **Sarde in saor** Sardines
marinated in a sweet and sour sauce
with sultanas and pine nuts.

➔ **Moeche** A Venetian delicacy
equivalent to truffles: soft-shelled
crabs fried in an egg batter and
served with a squeeze of lemon.

➔ **Risi e bisi** Springtime risotto
with peas and pancetta, sometimes
enhanced with Prosecco and
Stracchino cheese.

➔ **Risotto al nero di seppia**
Classic Venetian risotto, stained
black with cuttlefish ink; rice and
fish are braised in ink, wine and
a little tomato. Parmesan is not
added.

➔ **Frìtole alla Veneziana** Deep
fried doughnuts stuffed with rum-
or grappa-soaked raisins and pine
nuts, served during Carnival.

Left: Stored blocks
of Parmigiano

EMILIA—ROMAGNA

Emilia—Romagna sits at the heart of Italy, both geographically and gastronomically. Sandwiched between the Alps and Apennines, the region occupies an invisible food line between the creamy, cheesy, meat—obsessed north and the lighter, fruitier palate of the south, with its peppery olive oils and sweet tomatoes.

THE CHEESE LINE

Emilia-Romagna's capital, Bologna, certainly lives off the fat of the land. It's situated in a gorgeous green plain, the Pianura Padana, through which runs the River Po, making the soil perfect for fruit, vegetables, cereal crops and grazing. Follow the river east to the Po Delta and the Adriatic Sea supplies an abundance of game birds, fish and seafood. The region is also home to some of Italy's finest producers of cereals, pasta, parmesan, pork and balsamic vinegar, boasting 200 legally protected traditional products, 26 of which have IGP status.

Despite being joined into a single region, there are discernible differences between northwest

Emilia and southeast Romagna. The former, encompassing the cities of Bologna, Piacenza, Parma, Reggio Emilia, Modena and Ferrara, shares some gastronomic traditions with the north. Pork is the signature meat here – including Parma's famous prosciutto and *culatello*; Bologna's mortadella; Piacenza's pancetta and *coppa*; Ferrara's *salame da sugo*; and Modena's *zampone* and *cotechino* – and rice and polenta are eaten here too, albeit to a lesser extent than in the far north of Italy. Egg-based and stuffed pastas are popular, particularly tortelloni, cappelletti and lasagne, along with gnocchi, which is usually fried.

Southeastern Romagna, which encompasses Cesena, Faenza, Forlì, Imola, Ravenna and Rimini, enjoys a long stretch of Italy's eastern coastline. Food here features less meat and dairy and more seafood and olive oil. Rimini's *brodetto* (a hearty fish stew) is typical, as are dishes incorporating the region's excellent clams, while *canocchie* (mantis shrimps) are a seasonal treat. The alarmingly named *strozzapreti* ('priest-strangler') pasta is also Romagnolo, originating in local anti-clerical feeling when Romagna was a papal state. *Passatelli* is another regional pasta made from a dough

BOLOGNA certainly LIVES OFF the fat of THE LAND

of parmesan, breadcrumbs and cream cheese; it's served with a vegetable ragù. Forest delights such as chestnuts and truffles are also available in the mountains, along with the autumn conserve *savòr*, made with quinces, apples, pears, nuts (including almonds, hazelnuts and walnuts) and *saba* (*mosto cotto*), the grape reduction used as the base for balsamic. One of Romagna's most famous foods is undoubtedly the Eastern-influenced flatbread, *piadina*.

RAGÙ ALLA BOLOGNESE

If you come to Emilia-Romagna in search of 'authentic' spaghetti bolognese, you'll be out of luck. The name is a misnomer. Spaghetti bolognese is not Italian, and Bologna's fiercely traditional trattorias never list it. Instead, the city prides itself on a vastly superior meat-based sauce called ragù, consisting of slow-cooked minced pork belly and beef simmered with pancetta, onions, celery and carrots, and enriched with tomato paste, red wine and milk.

The accepted urban myth is that British and American servicemen fell in love with the local ragù when stationed in Bologna during WWII. When they returned home after the war, they asked immigrant Italian chefs to recreate the dish; however, the chefs weren't from Emilia-Romagna, so critical details were lost – resulting in a dish that is fundamentally different. Spaghetti bolognese is heavy on tomatoes, while ragù is all about the meat. Spaghetti is a dried Neapolitan pasta made from durum wheat, while Bologna's silky egg-based tagliatelle allows the unctuous meat sauce to stick to it. Ever keen to safeguard their meat sauce from mediocrity, Bologna's chamber of commerce registered an official ragù recipe in 1982.

ITALY'S FOODIE THEME PARK

The world's largest agri-food park, 7km (4 miles) northeast of Bologna's Piazza Maggiore, Fabbrica Italiana Contadina (aka FICO Eataly World) opened in 2017 to equal parts cheering and sneering. Love it or hate it, this 100,000 sq metre (1,076,391 sq ft) culinary theme park is a gastronomic juggernaut. It features 45 restaurants, including ventures from the likes of Michelin-starred chef Enrico Bartolini and Trattoria da Amerigo, itself a detour-worthy restaurant in Emilia-Romagna's truffle territory. It also includes endless speciality shops and kiosks, as well as wine and beer sections. A host of premium products are made on site, and there are workshops and demos covering pasta making, Parmigiano Reggiano, gelato, mortadella and more. Agricultural enthusiasts might enjoy the livestock areas, gardens and other agri-centric exhibitions. It's best to think of it as a kind of Disneyland for lovers of Italian food – a one-stop Holy Grail for the culinarily curious.

Left: Bolognese pasta sauce is always served locally with taglietelle Below: The Piazza Grande and Duomo Cathedral at sunset

ITALY'S BEST FOOD TOWN

Modena would easily make a top 10 list of best Italian culinary towns. The municipal market, Mercato Albinelli, is outstanding, its stalls heaving with Bible-sized hunks of Parmigiano Reggiano, bottles of aged balsamic vinegar and piles of fresh produce. Then there is Acetaia Giusti, established in 1605 and still Modena's best producer of balsamic vinegar. It offers six hour-long English-language tours daily, which include tastings. Finally, if you want to eat at Osteria Francescana, considered by many to be Italy's best restaurant, you'll need to reserve months in advance. Owner Massimo Bottura is onto his third Michelin star, and Francescana claimed the top spot on the influential World's 50 Best Restaurants list in 2016 and 2018.

Don't Miss

- **Anolini in brodo** Hailing from Piacenza, these are pasta pockets filled with meat, parmesan and breadcrumbs, swimming in a rich broth-like soup.
- **Cotechino di Modena** Pork sausage stuffed with seasoned mince and braised in Lambrusco wine; it's usually paired with lentils and mashed potatoes.
- **Tagliatelle al ragù** Thick, meat-heavy sauce served with egg-based tagliatelle.

- **Cappellacci di zucca** Ravioli-like pasta stuffed with pumpkin and nutmeg, and brushed with butter and sage.
- **Piadina** Thick, unleavened flatbread stuffed with rocket, tomato and local soft Squacquerone cheese.
- **Zuppa Inglese** An Italian trifle layered with cream, chocolate and *savoiardi* biscuits, and flavoured with Italian liqueur Alchermes.

TUSCANY

Tuscan cuisine was conjured up above an open wood fire in *la cucina contadina* (the farmer's kitchen). The basic premise of the region's cooking, which still holds true today, is simple: don't waste a crumb.

A COUNTRY KITCHEN

For centuries, the Italian aristocracy and clergy claimed the best cuts of meat, the freshest seafood and the finest produce, leaving all other Italians to make do with the scraps. Nowhere was this more true than in Tuscany where, in the 16th and 17th centuries, rich merchants and families such as the infamous Medici laid on elaborate banquets while ordinary Tuscans made do with dishes such as *acquacotta*, a simple soup made with stale bread, water and vegetables. As a result, contemporary Tuscan cuisine remains faithful to its humble roots, championing fresh local produce and eschewing fussy execution.

This philosophy also makes perfect sense in a region blessed with a wealth of fresh fruit and vegetables. Outstanding produce is the cornerstone of Tuscan cooking. Pulses, grains and beans sit at the heart of most daily meals, accompanied by wild fennel, black celery (braised as a side dish), sweet red onions (delicious when oven-roasted) and courgette flowers (stuffed and oven-baked), as well as artichokes, black cabbage, broad beans, chicory, chard, thistle-like cardoons and red and green tomatoes. Of huge local pride to farmers in the Garfagnana is the local *farro della garfagnana* (spelt), an ancient grain grown in Europe as early as 2500 BCE.

MEAT LOVERS

Tuscan markets conjure up animal parts many wouldn't dream of eating. In the past, offal was the staple peasant fare: tripe was simmered for hours with onions, carrots and herbs to make *lampredotto*, or with tomatoes and herbs to make *trippa alla Fiorentina* – two classics that are still going strong today, as is *pollo al mattone*, which featured on many a medieval fresco: boned chicken splattered beneath a brick, rubbed with herbs and baked beneath the brick. You're less likely to see ancient delicacies such as *cibrèo* (chicken's kidney, liver, heart and cockscomb stew) or *colle ripieno* (stuffed chicken's neck).

TUSCAN BREAD

Tuscan pane (bread) is deliberately unsalted to ensure that it lasts for a good week and to complement the region's salty cured meats. It forms the backbone of Tuscany's famous dishes: pappa al pomodoro *(bread and tomato soup),* panzanella *(tomato and basil salad mixed with bread soaked in cold water), and* ribollita *(a thick vegetable, bread and bean soup); the depth of flavour in these dishes is extraordinary.*

Left: The Chianti region
Right: Olive mill-style soup

In autumn, wild hare and boar also appear on the table, while the family pig invariably ends up on the plate as a salty slice of *soprassata* (head, skin and tongue boiled, chopped and flavoured with garlic, rosemary and other herbs and spices), or made into the familiar, wafer-thin prosciutto and the smooth, fat-speckled mortadella sausage. Other porky specialities include *finocchiona* (fennel-spiced sausage), San Miniato's *mallegato* (a near-black blood sausage spiked with nutmeg, cinnamon, raisins and pine kernels), and *lardo di Colonnata* (thin slices of pork fat aged in a mix of herbs and oils for at least six months), a delicacy that's hard to find outside Tuscany.

SUGAR AND SPICES

Be it the honey, almond and sugar-cane sweets served at the start of 14th-century Florentine banquets, the sugar sculptures at the 16th- and 17th-century feasts of the ruling Medici, or the humble *bomboloni* (doughnuts) sold by street vendors, Tuscan *dolci* (sweets) have always been reserved for festive occasions.

Legend has it that as far back as the 13th century, servants at the Abbazia di Montecelso near Siena paid tax to the nuns in the form of *panpepato* (a pepper and honey flatbread). Subsequently sweetened with spices, sprinkled with sugar and feasted on once a year at Christmas, Siena's *panforte* (literally 'strong bread') – a rich cake with nuts and candied fruit – is now eaten year-round. An adage says it stops couples from quarrelling.

Tuscan biscotti are dry, crisp and often double-baked. *Cantucci* are hard, sweet biscuits studded with almonds, while *brigidini di lamporecchio* are small, round aniseed-flavoured wafers; *ricciarelli* are almond biscuits, sometimes with candied oranges. In Lucca, locals are proud of their *buccellato* (a sweet bread with sultanas and aniseed seeds), a treat given by godparents to their godchild on their first Holy Communion and eaten with alacrity at all other times.

It was at the Florentine court of Catherine de' Medici that Italy's most famous dessert, gelato, first appeared, thanks to court maestro Bernardo Buontalenti (1531–1608), who engineered a way of freezing sweetened milk and egg yolks. For centuries afterwards, however, ice-cream and sherbets – a mix of shaved ice and fruit juice, served between courses at Renaissance banquets to aid digestion – only appeared on wealthy tables.

178

Don't Miss

- **Minestra di farro della Garfagnana** A soup made with chewy spelt flavoured with pancetta, potatoes and beans.
- **Panzanella** Water-soaked *pane sciocco* topped with chopped onion, tomato, cucumber and dressing.
- **Ribollita** A 'reboiled' bean, vegetable and bread soup with black cabbage that sits for a day before serving.

- **Pappardelle alla lepre** A typical Tuscan pasta, served with a wild hare ragù.
- **Cacciucco** The signature seafood stew of Livorno, made from five varieties of fish, simmered with tomatoes and red peppers and served atop stale bread.
- **Necci** Chestnut-flour pancakes filled with creamy ricotta and drizzled with honey.

BISTECCA ALLA FIORENTINA

The icon of Tuscan cuisine is Florence's *bistecca alla Fiorentina*, a chargrilled T-bone steak rubbed with olive oil, seared on the chargrill, seasoned and served *al sangue* (blue and bloody). This feisty cut of meat is weighed before being cooked, and priced on menus *per l'etto* (per 100g/3.5oz). Traditionally, it is butchered from Chianina cows, one of the world's oldest cattle breeds, which originate in the wide green Val di Chiana of eastern Tuscany.

UMBRIA

Mountainous Umbria is covered in wild woodlands and forest-cloaked uplands that provide ideal conditions for an array of mushrooms and truffles. Ever since the Etruscan era, the locals have hunted wild boar, foraged for black truffles and farmed ancient wheat varieties and the world's best lentils.

HUNTERS & FORAGERS

Once home to the ancient Etruscans, Umbria is still covered with dense forests that are gloriously green in spring and summer, and transform to a blanket of richly textured umber (hence the name) come autumn. Its wild woodlands and hillsides are full of roe deer, rabbits and wild boar, which continue to be hunted to provide the region's staples. Likewise, Lake Trasimeno – Umbria's only major lake – provides freshwater fish such as perch, eel, carp, pike and tench for a few hearty fish recipes.

There's no doubt that game takes pride of place on the Umbrian table. Tusked boar, wild hare (*lepre*) and venison flavour rich pasta dishes, while offal and off-cuts are fashioned into the region's legendary charcuterie.

Between October and March, many dishes feature the wood pigeons, woodcocks and doves which migrate through the region, alongside year-round staples such as quail, partridge and pheasant. Notable game bird dishes include *palombacci* (spit-roast wild doves glazed in a sauce of wine, garlic and capers) and *beccaccia alla norcina* (stuffed, spit-roast woodcocks).

Umbria's forests are known for their black truffles, found here in greater abundance than anywhere else in Italy. They can be foraged year-round, but are at their best in the summer months. In winter, the rarer and more expensive white truffle also makes a showing. Given their prevalence, truffles are used generously in Umbria: grated onto risottos, blended into cheese and folded into eggs. Mushrooms, too, are eagerly foraged in autumn, the best of them being the porcini.

LAST OF THE NORCINOS

Tucked away in Umbria's far eastern reaches, remote Norcia sends Italian gastronomes into raptures over the earthy delights of its *tartufo nero* (black truffles) and the salumi from its acorn-fed pigs and wild boar, both of which feature prolifically on restaurant menus and in shop windows. Umbria, and in particular Norcia, has been famous for its cured meats and pork since Roman

UMBRIA'S FORESTS are known for their BLACK TRUFFLES

times, when Norcia's butchers (*norcinos*) were sometimes called on to perform basic operations on people. These days, *norcinos* are recognised as the finest artisanal butchers in Italy, preparing pork products better than anyone else in the country.

Located near the Marche border, the area around Norcia is wild and unspoilt, characterised by the chestnut and oak forests favoured by wild boar (*cinghiale*), which love to feast on acorns and truffles. Boar is a lean meat like venison, and only some parts of the animal can be used, so the meat is expensive and reserved for the best sauces and superior prosciutto and salumi. For big feasts a whole boar might be spit-roast with wild herbs and garlic. Wander the sleepy streets of Norcia and you'll find family-owned butchers with *norcineria* written above the door – these are the last few master butchers who are keeping the *norcino* tradition alive.

CASTELLUCCIO LENTILS

In general, pulses are more popular than pasta in Umbria, and include ancient spelt and fagiolina del Trasimeno (a bean cultivated around Lake Trasimeno). But the star of the show here hails from the Castelluccio plains, just below the Sibillini mountains, where the fertile fields are used to cultivate what some say are the world's best lentils (lenticchie). These tiny brown gems are IGP protected and have such thin skins that they don't require soaking before cooking – they're tender enough to eat after simmering lightly for just 30 minutes, during which time they absorb the perfumes of whatever herbs, spices or aromatics are added to them, while retaining their own nutty flavour. They're perhaps best appreciated in a bowl of hearty zuppa di lenticchie.

Clockwise from left:
The town of Assisi;
Cappellacci with saffron
potatoes; The plains of
Castellucio, in Umbria;
A handful of truffles;
Strangozzi with Norcia
black truffle

Don't Miss

➔ **Zuppa di lenticchie** A ubiquitous lentil soup, built on a base of sautéed *soffritto* (finely chopped onion, celery and carrot) and enhanced with tomato concentrate and white wine.

➔ **Colombaccio** Slowly spit-roasted wood pigeon, served with a *salsa ghiotta* flavoured with the bird's liver.

➔ **Porchetta** An Umbrian original, this spit-roast pork is flavoured with fennel and garlic and popped into a bread roll.

➔ **Pasta alla Norcina** *Strangozzi* pasta served with a sauce of cream, white wine, sausage, mushrooms and truffles.

➔ **Tegamaccio** A simple stew filled with the day's fresh fish (perch, eel, carp or pike) and flavoured with tomatoes, white wine, parsley and olive oil.

➔ **Torcolo** A ring-shaped cake filled with pine nuts, raisins, citrus peel and candied fruits.

LE MARCHE

Like Umbria, Le Marche is a largely mountainous region with a thin sliver of coastline along its eastern edge. Inland, flavourful stews, grilled and roasted meats and salumi such as *ciauscolo* (a soft, spreadable sausage) are the standard. In fact, the citizens of Le Marche eat more meat per capita than in any other part of Italy.

Aside from meat, simple soups containing vegetables and pulses are the order of the day. *Minestra di ceci alla Marchigiana* is a classic example, a chickpea, tomato, celery and spinach soup enhanced with Parma ham. The local prosciutto is *di Carpegna*, flavoured with juniper. Soups are also popular along the coast, where seafood takes over as the staple. Recipes differ according to each town, but the most famous is *brodetto all'Anconetana*, from the regional capital Ancona, which traditionally features thirteen different types of fish and seafood.

FRITTO MISTO

Deep-frying is a popular method of preparation in Le Marche – a typical *fritto misto* (mixed fry up) here includes a variety of breaded or battered meat and vegetables, served on a large platter. The most famous of the region's fried treats are *olive all'Ascolana*, a delectable street food from Ascoli Piceno, which produces some of Italy's best olives; the fried version sees them stuffed with meat, covered in breadcrumbs and deep-fried. Even more strange is the *crema fritta*, deep-fried cream, a centuries-old regional dish. Usually served as a starter alongside other *fritto misto*, the cream is set before being cut into diamond shapes, battered and deep fried. The sweet flavour offsets the bitter olives.

MACCHERONCINI DI CAMPOFILONE

Le Marche's gastronomic treasure is maccheroncini di Campofilone *pasta, first made in the early 15th century and, in 2013, the first egg pasta to become IGP protected. Made without any water, the pasta dough contains ten eggs per kilo of flour (which must be made from Le Marche grains). It is then rolled very long, cut very thin (1mm strands) and left to dry slowly at 36°C (97°F), which enables the pasta to be preserved for long periods of time despite its high egg content. Typically,* maccheroncini di Campofilone *was served with a sauce of chicken giblets or meat ragù, and has an incredible melt-in-the-mouth texture.*

Don't Miss

→ **Olive all'Ascolana** Meat-stuffed olives from Ascoli Piceno, covered in breadcrumbs and deep-fried.

→ **Casciotta d'Urbino** A very old, semi-hard, DOP-protected sheep's cheese, said to have been favoured by Michelangelo.

→ **Brodetto all'Anconetana** A tomato and garlic based stew incorporating cuttlefish, shellfish, prawns, crayfish, cod, mullet, sole, gurnard, flounder, scorpionfish and calamari.

→ **Vincisgrassi** A lasagne-style dish layering pasta sheets with a ragù of beef, pork, sweetbreads and chicken livers and hearts.

→ **Coniglio in porchetta** Rabbit stuffed with fennel, garlic and cured pork, seared and then roasted in the oven with white wine.

→ **Ricotta calcioni** Parcels of shortcrust pastry filled with sweet ricotta and lemon peel, deep-fried and sprinkled with lemon zest and honey.

LAZiO

Dominated by the vivacious, food-loving capital of Rome, the wider region of Lazio is often overlooked. That's a shame given the wealth of produce from its long coast, vast agricultural plains, vine-covered volcanic slopes and fish-filled lakes and rivers.

ROBUST, RURAL FLAVOURS

Situated slap-bang in the centre of the Italian peninsula and bordered by the great food regions of Tuscany to the north and Campania to the south, Lazio shares its neighbours' love of honest, rural ingredients and robust flavours. The region is also blessed with a huge variety of quality products from land, sea, lake, hillsides, rivers and marshes. Here you'll find the best artichokes in Italy (*mammole* and *cimaroli* – large, round and completely without thorns), as well as sweet peppers and fragrant lettuce with long crunchy leaves. Look out, too, for green beans from Lago di Bracciano, white and sweet onions from Marino, delicate peas from Frosinone, scatoloni beans from Accumoli, and cannellini beans

from Atina, Bolsena and Viterbo. Chickpeas, too, are ubiquitous and served in stews and broths.

Meat is highly prized here, particularly lamb and pork. The latter is used for cured meats, pancetta and the *guanciale* (pork jowl) found in two of the region's most famous pasta dishes, *bucatini all'Amatriciana* and the more well-known carbonara. Keep an eye out, too, for mortadella from Amatrice. Italy's most famous meat dish, saltimbocca, also hails from Lazio. The authentic version is made with pieces of veal wrapped in thin slices of prosciutto and sage leaves, before being pan-fried in white wine and butter. Porchetta, boneless roast pork stuffed into bread rolls, is one of the region's most popular street foods.

UNMISSABLE LAZIAN FOOD EXPERIENCES

Il Granchio, Terracina One of the best seafood restaurants on the Lazian coast, serving unusual market finds such as *ricciola* (amberjack), red prawns and squid-ink ravioli stuffed with cod, cauliflower and pistachio.

Street stalls, Castel Gandolfo Handsome Castel Gandolfo overlooks Lago Albano, where the Pope has his summer

'ANGRY' PASTA

With a name that translates literally as 'angry' (in reference to its fiery chilli content) arrabbiata is a tomato-based Lazian pasta sauce, with added garlic and basil for an aromatic finish. It's usually served without cheese, making it naturally vegan.

residence, and its streets are dotted with food stalls selling porchetta, pecorino cheese and pickles – you can sit down and eat them at local canteens for a nominal cover charge (around €5 including bread and half a litre of wine).

Cacciani, Frascati This renowned Frascati restaurant offers regional classics and twinkling terrace views. Look out for *tonnarello a cacio e pepe*, egg spaghetti with pecorino cheese and black pepper.

LAZIAN WINES

White wines dominate Lazio's production – 95% of the region's DOC wines are white. Most restaurant house whites will be from the Castelli Romani area to the southeast of Rome, centred on Frascati and Marino. New production techniques have led to a lighter, drier wine that is beginning to be taken seriously: Frascati Superiore is now an excellent tipple, and Castel de Paolis' Vigna Adriana wins plaudits, while the emphatically named Est! Est!! Est!!! is increasingly drinkable; it's produced by venerable wine house Falesco, based in Montefiascone on the volcanic banks of Lago Bolsena.

Left: The fountains of Villa d'Este in Tivoli
Top: Veal cutlets

© Jay Boivin / Getty Images; © Susan Wright / Lonely Planet

Don't Miss

➔ **Bucatini all'Amatriciana** Fat spaghetti with a hollow centre, dressed with a *guanciale*, onion and tomato sauce. Typical of Amatrice.

➔ **Stracci di Antrodoco** Thin crepes, stuffed with beef ragù and topped with tomatoes and parmesan before being baked. A speciality of Rieti province.

➔ **Bazzoffia** A soup of fresh fava beans, peas, artichokes and curly escarole enriched with croutons and eggs, typical of southern Lazio.

➔ **Ciriole con piselli** Little eels cooked in a skillet with fresh peas.

➔ **Carciofi alla matticella** Artichokes flavoured with garlic, mint, olive oil and salt and roasted over a grate, typical of Velletri.

➔ **Budino di ricotta** Pudding consisting of ricotta, candied orange and lemon peel, cinnamon and rum.

ROME

Food feeds the Roman soul. The Lazio province's capital lives to eat, and the city's restaurant scene has become increasingly sophisticated. Nonetheless, traditional no-frills trattorias still provide Rome's most memorable gastronomic experiences.

THE FIFTH QUARTER

Many of Rome's classic dishes speak of an impoverished people. Even during the heyday of Roman rule here, up to third of the city's inhabitants were given a bread ration to prevent them from starving; and right up to the 20th century, Rome operated a system whereby meat was distributed according to social class. At the slaughterhouse (*mattatoio*), animals were broken down into quarters, depending on quality. The *primo quarto* (first quarter) consisted of prime cuts and was allocated to the nobility, the second quarter was for the clergy, the third quarter went to the bourgeois and the fourth to the army. The rest of Rome was left with the *quinto quarto* (fifth quarter) – the leftovers, including feet, tails, brains and innards.

The best place to sample these oft-maligned cuts is in the *trattorie* of Testaccio, a traditional working-class district clustered around the city's former abattoir. In the past, butchers who worked here were often paid partly in cheap cuts of meat – the superb Roman staple of *coda alla vaccinara* translates as 'oxtail cooked butcher's style'; it's simmered for hours to create a rich sauce with tender slivers of meat. A famous Roman dish that's not for the faint-hearted is pasta with *pajata*, made with the entrails of young veal calves, considered a delicacy since they contain the mother's congealed milk. If you see the word *coratella* in a dish, it means you'll be eating lungs, kidneys and hearts.

ROMAN CUISINE

Cucina romana (Roman cooking) was born of careful use of local ingredients – making use of the cheaper cuts of meat, like *guanciale* (pig's cheek), and greens (*misticanze*) that could be gathered wild from the fields. There are a few classic Roman pasta dishes that almost every trattoria and restaurant in the city will serve. These carb-laden comfort foods are seemingly simple yet notoriously difficult to prepare well, and include *carbonara* (pasta with *guanciale*, egg and salty sheep's-milk Pecorino Romano), *alla gricia* (with *guanciale* and onions), *Amatriciana* (invented when a chef from Amatrice added tomatoes to *alla gricia*) and *cacio*

From top: Sizzling veal escalopes; Bar restaurant in Trastevere; Chefs outside a restaurant in Rome

e pepe (with Pecorino Romano and black pepper).

Other Roman specialities include *baccalà con i ceci* (salted cod with chickpeas) and *trippa alla Romana* (tripe stewed in a tomato sauce and topped with pecorino).

ROMAN GREENS

Despite their love of meaty dishes, Romans enjoy a wide variety of healthy greens year-round. Grass-green *fava* beans are an essential element in the countryside picnics that Roman workers traditionally enjoy on May Day public holiday; and early summer is also when the green, fluted *zucchine romanesche* (Roman courgettes) are sold complete with their flowers, which are usually stuffed and deep-fried. *Melanzane* (aubergine) is a big summertime treat, as are leafy greens such as the sturdy and flavourful Roman lettuce, *lattuga romana*. In autumn, markets heave with mushrooms – the meaty porcini, *galletti* and *ovuli* – and long-stemmed *broccoletti* (also called *broccolini*). Even in winter, you can tuck into hearty vegetable minestrones, filled out with fresh *ceci* (chickpeas).

JEWISH SPECIALITIES

Between the 16th and 19th centuries, Rome's Jewish population was confined to the city's ghetto, and their ebraico-romanesca (Jewish-Roman) food traditions remain deeply entrenched in the area. To add flavour to limited ingredients – those spurned by the rich, such as courgette flowers – they began to deep-fry everything from mozzarella to salt cod (baccalà). Particularly addictive are the locally grown artichokes, which are flattened out to form a kind of flower shape, deep-fried to a golden crisp and then salted to become carciofo alla giudia.

Don't Miss

➲ **Spaghetti alla carbonara** The most famous Roman pasta dish, made with *guanciale* (cured pig's cheek), eggs and pecorino cheese.

➲ **Carciofi alla Romana** Artichokes stuffed with parsley, mint and garlic, then braised in broth and white wine.

➲ **Vignarola** A springtime stew of fresh artichokes, broad beans and peas cooked in white wine and lemon juice.

➲ **Pollo alla Romana** A whole jointed chicken, braised in wine with tomatoes, peppers and oregano.

➲ **Saltimbocca alla Romana** Pan-fried veal escalopes, wrapped with prosciutto and sage and finished in white wine.

FOOD & WINE TOURS

Casa Mia Food and wine tours for serious gastronomes, with tastings and behind-the-scenes meetings with local shopkeepers, producers, chefs and restaurateurs. www.casamiatours.com

Katie Parla The author of the city's best-known English-language food blog also conducts private walking tours for small groups. www.katieparla.com

The Tour Guy Foodie tours in Trastevere with this young, fun tour company. www.theromanguy.com

Elizabeth Minchilli Small-group food tours, with tastings, of Campo de' Fiori market and the Jewish Ghetto, Testaccio and Monti. www.elizabethminchilli.com

Vino Roma Serious wine-tasting classes in a specialist tasting studio in Monti. www.vinoroma.com

Left: Artichokes Roman style

ABRUZZO & MOLISE

Hunkered between the Apennine Mountains to the west and the Adriatic Sea to the east, the neighbouring regions of Abruzzo and Molise are still rural and unspoilt, featuring a robust, rustic cuisine based on age-old agricultural methods, simple ingredients and homely culinary traditions.

BETWEEN SEA AND MOUNTAIN

Set across the spiny ridge of the Apennine Mountains, nearly half of the region is given over to national park, and a wild, unspoilt feel dominates here. Inland, shepherds watch over huge flocks of sheep and (to a lesser extent) goats, while along the Adriatic Coast fisherfolk hang out on *trabocchi* (*travocchi* in local dialect), ancient fishing piers equipped with a winch and nets hung on extended wooden arms, which intercept shoals of fish. *Trabocchi* sometimes feature a small hut, which can serve as an impromptu seasonal restaurant.

Whether you're sitting beachside or in a mountain hamlet, the food on your plate will be humble and hearty, honouring the best local ingredients. Lamb is big here, served braised, roasted over a wood fire, fried or in pasta sauces. The region's sheep spend the spring grazing on the wildflowers and herbs in the high pastures, which lends an intense flavour to their meat. *Arrosticini* is a classic Abbruzzese dish: skewers of local lamb, seasoned with salt, pepper, rosemary and olive oil, and cooked over a special barbecue until meltingly tender. They're served with pickles and a glass of the local Montepulciano d'Abru-

zzo red wine. Otherwise, lamb is cooked with the ubiquitous local *diavolino* ('little devil') chillies, or in a ragù with *chitarra* egg pasta. In Molise, offal-based specialities such as *abbuoti* (baked parcels of lamb's liver, sweetbreads and egg) and *torcinelli* (lamb's liver sausages cooked over coals) are also very popular.

On the coast, lamb gives way to salt cod, seafood and fish, particularly the tasty and cheap silvery-blue anchovies (*alici or acciughe*) that are the favourite of local fisherfolk – a healthy preference given the anchovy's high content of omega-3-rich oils. *Acciughe* caught along the Adriatic coast are considered more delicate than the plumper, fatter variety fished in the Tyrrhenian Sea, and those from Vasto are considered the very best. Vasto's anchovy frittata is a celebrated dish, combining the fish with eggs, chilli flakes and pecorino cheese. Chieti, too, boasts a highlight anchovy *antipasto* of fried eggy bread topped with anchovy fillets and capers.

NAVELLI SAFFRON

Navelli is probably the richest village in Abruzzo thanks to its premium crop of saffron (*zafferano*). The pretty purple plant (*crocus sativa*) is thought to have been smuggled over from Spain in the 13th century by a Dominican monk – saffron was a valuable medicinal commodity at the time. But it was during the Renaissance that saffron became a gastronomic delicacy, thanks to the aristocratic families who used it to colour their food gold, most famously in Milan's *risotto alla Milanese*. It's still mainly exported out of the region, as Abruzzo's farmers have little use for such an expensive foodstuff, although you will find it in *scapece di Vasto*, a mixed seafood dish where floured and fried fish is marinated for a week in white-wine vinegar, saffron and white wine.

Navelli's saffron is of the highest quality, and has DOP status. It's grown in sticky, mineral-rich black soil by the 80 smallholders of the Altopiano Navelli co-operative, who cultivate a tiny area of just 8 hectares (20 acres) and harvest the saffron by hand at the end of October. The yellow stigmas are still collected for medical purposes, while the orange stamens are toasted over hot walnut or almond coals. During this process they lose around 80% of their weight, which means some 200,000 flowers and 500 hours of work are required to make 1kg of dried saffron. The disused petals are used to refertilise the soil, which cannot be replanted with saffron for a decade.

MOLISE PASTA

Molise is the heart of the region's wheat-growing territory and is notable for its pasta-making traditions. Its signature pastas are fusilli and the lesser-known cavatelli, *that looks something like a miniature hot-dog roll. Both were traditionally hand-made, the corkscrew of fusilli achieved winding strips of pasta around a spindle. Fusilli is typically served with peppery lamb ragù, cavatelli with sausage and the broccoli-like rapini/turnip green (rapa) in the classic Molisani dish* cavatelli con salsiccia e cime di rapa. Cappellacci *is another popular Molise pasta, little pouches stuffed with local cheeses, while the rarest pasta is that made with so-called 'pharaoh's wheat',* saragolla, *a grain that arrived in Europe around 632 CE.*

Don't Miss

- **Pizza scima** A golden, crunchy, thick flat bread similar to focaccia; it's also called pizza *scema*, *scive* or *acime*.
- **Fiadoni** A small baked pastry stuffed with a mix of ricotta and pecorino, sometimes with bacon or chilli.
- **Centerbe** Abruzzo's iconic, bright green liqueur is based on an ancient Benedictine recipe incorporating a hundred wild herbs.
- **Cavatelli con sugo di ventricina** Cavatelli pasta with a tomato sauce of *ventricina* salumi, fennel and garlic.
- **Arrosticini** Skewers of lamb seasoned with salt, pepper, oil and rosemary and cooked over a wood fire.
- **Brodetto Vastese** A fish stew, with six or seven types of fish and shellfish cooked in a terracotta pot with garlic, herbs and cherry tomatoes.

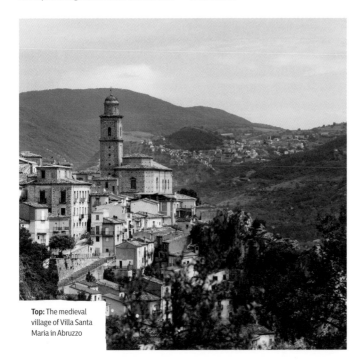

Top: The medieval village of Villa Santa Maria in Abruzzo

LITTLE DEVILS

In some restaurants in Abruzzo, the place setting may include a pair of scissors, supplied so that you can snip bits of locally grown chilli into whatever you're eating. Fondly known as diavolini *('little devils'), these chillies have a sweet, piquant taste rather than being too fiery. They are cut fresh over food, preserved in olive oil, or dried and crushed into chilli flakes which are used, like pepper, to season meat, vegetable and fish stews. Diavolini are the key element in the region's signature salumi, ventricina, a cured pork sausage that's also flavoured with bell peppers, black pepper and fennel. The Abruzzese love of chillies is celebrated each year in the town of Filetto, which hosts a four-day chilli festival during the third week of August.*

CAMPANIA

Everything tastes better in Campania, where food, identity and pride are inseparable. Some put it down to the volcanic soil, others to the region's sun and soulfulness. But whatever the reason, eating in Campania is a mouthwatering experience.

HIGH AND LOW TABLES

Campania's showstopping cuisine is an exotic culmination of foreign influence and local resourcefulness. The Romans valued the region for its vast pastures and rich volcanic soils, and many of today's dearly held traditions date right back to the Romans. The ancient towns of Amalfi, Cetara and Positano started life as Roman fishing villages, and many of their inhabitants still make a living from the sea. As foreigners have come and gone over the centuries, they've also left their mark. The ancient Greeks brought olive trees, grapevines and durum wheat, while the Byzantines and Arabs brought pine nuts, almonds, raisins and honey, as well as Italy's most famous food – pasta.

During Naples' Bourbon period (1734–1860), two parallel gastronomic cultures developed: that of the opulent Spanish monarchy, and that of the streets – the *cucina povera* (cuisine of the poor). As much as the former was elaborate and rich, the latter was simple and healthy. The food of the poor – the so-called *mangiafoglie* (leaf eaters) – was largely based on pasta, and on vegetables grown on the fertile volcanic plains around Naples. Aubergines (eggplants), artichokes, courgettes (zucchini), tomatoes and peppers were among the staples, while milk from sheep, cows and goats was used to make cheese. Flatbreads imported from Greek and Arab lands, the forebears of pizza, were also popular. Meat and fish were expensive, and reserved for special occasions.

Meanwhile, in the court kitchens, the top French cooks of the day were working to feed the insatiable appetites of the Bourbon monarchy. The headstrong queen Maria Carolina, wife of King Ferdinand I, was so impressed by her sister Marie Antoinette's court in Versailles that she asked to borrow some chefs. These Gallic imports took to the Neapolitan air, creating such delights as the highly elaborate *timballo di pasta* (pasta pies), the *gattò di patate* (potato tart) and the iconic *babà*, a mushroom-shaped sponge cake soaked in rum and sugar.

AN EXOTIC culmination OF FOREIGN iNFLUENCE and local RESOURCEFULNESS

SOUTHERN STAPLES

Beyond pizza Napoletana – which has STG (Specialità Tradizionale Garantita; Guaranteed Traditional Speciality) status and is listed as an 'Intangible Cultural Heritage of Humanity' by Unesco – the city is known for its fragrant pastries and *fritture* (fried snacks). Its bounty of staples also includes the world-famous *pizza margherita*, *pizza di scarola* (endive or escarole pie), Napoli salami, wild-fennel sausages and *sanguinaccio* (a cream of candied fruits and chocolate, made during Carnevale). In the Campi Flegrei district, Pozzuoli has a lively fish market and another Campi Flegrei highlight is the IGP-certified Annurca apple, ripened on a bed of straw to produce the fruit's distinctively striped red hue.

Seafood revelations are the norm on the Amalfi Coast, from cod and monkfish to grey mullet and *coccio* (rockfish), and on the off-shore islands of Procida, Ischia and Capri. On Procida, local concoctions include anchovy-stuffed squid and *volamarina* (moonfish) tripe with tomato and chilli, while the agricultural history of neighbouring Ischia shines through in classics like *coniglio all'Ischitana*, a stew made with locally bred rabbits. Almonds and chocolate are key ingredients of the sugar-dusted *torta Caprese*

cake which, alongside seafood dishes like linguine in scorpion-fish sauce and the refreshing Caprese salad, hail from the island of Capri.

The Sorrento peninsula is home to gnocchi *alla Sorrentina* (gnocchi baked in a mozzarella-laced tomato sauce) and refreshing limoncello sorbet. Feast on *burrino incamiciato* (cow's milk mozzarella, wickedly filled with butter), pizza-by-the-metre in Vico Equense, or ricotta-stuffed cannelloni in Sorrento. You'll also find Cetara's Colatura di Alici (an intense anchovy essence), and Colline Salernitane DOP olive oil from Salerno.

Further south, the rural Cilento region expresses more earthy tendencies in *cuccia* (a soup of chickpeas, lentils, maize, wheat and the ancient *cicerchia* legume) and *pastorelle* (a fried puff-pastry treat filled with chestnut custard).

THE SWEET LIFE

Fragrant *sfogliatelle* (cinnamon-infused pastries with ricotta and candied fruit) and *babà* aren't the only sweets you'll find in Campania. *Torta di ricotta e pera* (a tangy ricotta and pear torte) and limoncello-flavoured *delizia al limone* cake are also ubiquitous. *Cassatina* is the Neapolitan version of the Sicilian *cassata*, made with *pan di Spagna* (Italian sponge), ricotta and candied fruit, while the latticed *pastiera* (a shortcrust pastry tart filled with ricotta, candied fruit and cereals, and flavoured with orange-blossom water) is an Easter tradition. *Paste reali* are miniature fruit and vegetables cleverly crafted from marzipan at Christmas, when sponge-and-marzipan *raffioli* biscuits are also served.

Don't Miss

- **Insalata Caprese** One of the world's greatest salads, a classic and simple assembly of the very best Mozzarella di Bufala with tomatoes and fresh basil.
- **Pizza Margherita** It's hard to overemphasise the cultural importance of this eternally popular pizza, topped with tomato sauce, fresh basil and cheese.
- **Sfogliatelle** So-called 'lobster tails': crispy layered pastry with a sweet semolina and ricotta filling.

- **Polipetti affogati** A traditional dish of baby octopus braised in a garlic- and chilli-infused tomato sauce.
- **Pasta alla Sorrentina** Sorrento is the home of the large, tubular cannelloni, which is typically served with tomato, basil and mozzarella.
- **Spaghetti alle vongole** Spaghetti with clams cooked in white wine, one of Campania's most popular dishes.

PASTA & THE FORK

Although it was first introduced in the 12th century, pasta only really took off in the 17th century when it became established as the poor man's food of choice. Requiring only a few simple ingredients – just flour and water at its most basic – pasta proved a lifesaver when the population of Naples exploded. The nobility, however, continued to shun it until Gennaro Spadaccini invented the four-pronged fork in the early 18th century, making it possible to eat pasta with a degree of elegance.

From left: A small food shop in Naples; pizza from Pizziera Bellini

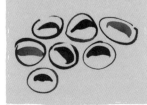

PUGLIA

The food of Puglia is rooted in its history of hard times: pasta made without eggs, bread from hard durum wheat, wild greens foraged from the countryside. This is honest, tasty home-cooking – delicious, but driven by necessity.

POOR MAN'S FOOD

The cuisine of Puglia is *la cucina povera* (poor man's food), originally created by struggling farmers and fisherfolk – food historian Luigi Sada describes *zuppa di pesce fuggito* ('fish soup from which the fish has fled') as consisting just of seashells boiled with basil, oil and vermicelli. The tradition of *sopratavola* – raw vegetables such as fennel or chicory, eaten after a meal – arose simply because people here could not afford to round off a meal with fruit.

But that doesn't mean that food isn't taken seriously here, nor that the Pugliese devote little time or effort to what's on their plates. The local cuisine may not be sophisticated, but it is hyper-local, seasonal and full of flavour. Take, for example, pan-roasted peppers and almonds served with homemade bread; or *cime di rapa*, a puree of broad beans and rapa (rapini/broccoli rabe) drizzled with fresh olive oil. While fish and seafood are the staples along the coast, meat is still seen as something of a treat, and beef is unusual; chicken, rabbit and lamb are the traditional meats of the region, while *cavallo* (horse meat) is a more recent addition.

Waves of conquest and immigration over the centuries have introduced new foodstuffs and left their mark on flavours. The Swabians brought radishes, the Arabs citrus fruits, juniper, raisins and almonds, and the Spanish tomatoes and potatoes. Many dishes also taste distinctly Greek along this east-facing southern seaboard, such as *polpo in umido* (stewed octopus) or *polpo alla pignata* (octopus steamed with

ENOTRIA

The Greeks called Puglia Enotria ('Wine Land'), but until the 1980s, the region's strong wines were considered unrefined, and were generally use to provide body and strength to blends of north Italian and French wines. These days, however, winemakers such as Antinori and Avignonesi are investing here and introducing more modern practices. Given the strength of the sun, it is the reds that earn most plaudits, based on Primitivo (a clone of Zinfandel), Negroamaro, Nero di Troia and Malvasia grapes. Primitivi and Negroamaro are often blended to get the best results from the sweet Primitivo and the slightly bitter edge of Negroamaro.

garlic, onion, tomatoes, parsley, olive oil, bay leaves and cinnamon). And it was the Greeks who planted Puglia's ancient olive trees, which are now protected by law. It's said there are 50 million of them today, and together they produce 40% of Italy's olive oil.

BREAD AND PASTA

In Puglia, eating a meal without bread is like playing tennis without a racquet – for a start, you'll need it to wipe up the sauce, a practice called *fare scarpetta* ('to make a little shoe'). Bread here is usually made from hard durum wheat, and has a russet-brown crust, an almost eggy-golden interior and distinctively good flavour. It's baked in wood-burning ovens, and keeps well. Puglia's most famous DOP-protected bread comes from Altamura, and is made with ingredients and techniques almost unchanged since the bakers' guild was formed in the Middle Ages. It is thrice-risen and improves with time.

Many Puglian recipes also call for breadcrumbs made from stale bread – *pane rafferme* ('firmed-up bread'). *Friselle*, bagel-shaped rolls that have been dried, are another Pugliese delicacy born out of practicality, ideal for labourers on the move; they are doused in water to soften and then dressed with tomatoes, olive oil and oregano. *Taralli* are like an Italian pretzel and come plain in Bari, sprinkled with fennel seeds in Taranto and with a little chilli in Lecce.

Given Puglia's large-scale cultivation of durum wheat, the region is also famous for its many pasta styles. The best known is the *orecchiette* ('little ears') fresh pasta, which you'll often see people making outside their homes. Other shapes include *tapparelle* ('large ears'), *troccoli* (a kind of thick spaghetti), *sagne* (ribbons of fettucine) and *capunti* (short, oval-shaped and a little like an open pea-pod). *Minchiareddhri* is a cylindrical pasta made with barley flour, while *tria* is a large, flat, handmade pasta combined with chickpeas in a soup.

Left from top: A harbourside catch; The white town in Apulia; A chicory & broad bean puree

FRUITS OF THE SEA

One of the highlights of coastal tables in April are the 'fruits of the sea', ricci di mare (sea urchins). All along the coast south of Bari you'll see signs emblazoned with 'ricci' and crowds gathered at rustic restaurants where trays are piled high with the prickly delicacy. Once they're cracked open, you dip bread into the delicate, dark-red roe, although many Pugliese simply slurp the contents down like oysters. Ricci are only in season for a short period as the eggs are eventually ejected. Other popular Pugliese seafood includes octopus, cuttlefish, squid and mussels.

Don't Miss

➡ **Burrata di Andria** A porcelain-white mozzarella filled with cream, which should ideally be eaten within 24 hours of being made.

➡ **Fave e cicoria** Fava beans mashed into a puree with wild chicory (or other greens) and drizzled with olive oil.

➡ **Friselle Salentine** Hard and crunchy bagel-shaped breads, rehydrated with water before being topped with olive oil and tomatoes.

➡ **Orecchiette con cime di rapa** Puglia's signature dish: fresh *orecchiette* pasta mixed with bitter rapa greens (also known as rapini or broccoli rabe).

➡ **Calzone di cipolla** Pizza-dough pie filled with tomatoes, olives, anchovies and the local *cipolle sponsali*, a sweet red onion.

➡ **Tiella** A baked pie of mussels in their shells, layered with potatoes, tomatoes and rice, topped with breadcrumbs and steamed in white wine.

BASILICATA

Basilicata is Italy's last true wilderness, a chaotic landscape of forested valleys and purple-hued, mist-wreathed mountains that remains mysterious and isolated. In this historically poor region of unforgiving terrain, food is simple, honest and ancient, much of it based on Italy's oldest grains, legumes and vegetables.

THE GRAIN BELT

Nearly half of Basilicata is given over to the cultivation of grain, particularly wheat, which illustrates the historic importance of the crop given the dry, mountainous conditions in much of this tiny region. Durum wheat has been farmed here for thousands of years, and some of the varieties grown, such as Khorasan and Risciola, are among the oldest in Europe. Today, Basilicata can lay claim to a host of unique pasta shapes such as *lucane chiappute*, a sort of super-sized tagliatelle.

More famous still is Basilicata's huge variety of breads, of which *pane di Matera* is the oldest and most revered. Bread has been baked in the cliff-hewn town of Matera for as long as people have lived here – estimated to be at least 7000 years. With a lumpy, conical shape, this primitive looking loaf, with its hard, dark brown crust and pale yellow crumb, is made from the locally milled Senatore Cappelli semolina grain, and a natural yeast derived from grapes and figs fermented in local spring water. Traditionally, the dough was left to ferment in Matera's caves over long periods of time, resulting in bread not dissimilar to sourdough. It's eaten with everything from charcuterie and cheese to fresh vegetables and stews. Once stale, it's the key ingredient of the regional staple, tomato-based *pasta mollicata*, as well as of *acquasale*, a bread soup similar to Tuscany's *acquacotta*.

SENISE PEPPERS

Sweet, smoky peperone di Senise are harvested every August in the town of Senise, where they're hung out to dry in the summer sun on almost every balcony. Originating in the Antilles, the peppers arrived here from the New World in the 16th century when the Spanish controlled southern Italy. Although they look like chillies, they're sweet rather than hot. Fresh Senise peppers are sometimes used in soups and stews, but more usually they are dried and cooked in oil, to be served alongside fish or roasted meat; or crushed (cruschi) into a powder known as Basilicata gold.

NEW & OLD WORLD FLAVOURS

Alongside pasta and bread, you'll find many dishes featuring legumes like chickpeas. Tomatoes and peppers are other imports from this era, which now characterise regional cooking and feature in classic Basilicata dishes like *pignata di pecora* – mutton cooked in a clay pot (*pignata*) with potatoes, tomatoes, onions, port and pecorino cheese. Like Calabria, chillies (*peperoncino* or *diavulicciu*) also rear their head, and you'll spot more ancient Arab influences as well – raisins, pine nuts and even pomegranate – in dishes such as *grano dolce*, a pudding of wheat grains blended with chocolate, walnuts, pomegranate seeds and *vincotto* (sweet 'cooked wine'). Strangest of all, though, are the unique red aubergines from Rotonda, which look like tomatoes and were brought from Africa in the 19th century. They are bitter and slightly spicy, and are often dried, pickled or preserved in oil and served as *antipasti*.

MUTTON, CURED MEAT AND CHEESE

Basilicata has little room for grazing, so meat was (and still is) a valuable commodity, usually eaten in hearty stews such as *cutturiddi*, which is made with mutton rather than lamb. Dried and smoked meats are still prepared in the winter months; acorn-fed pigs, for example, are transformed into the local *lucanica* sausage – favoured by the Romans, its flavour was remarked upon by Apicius and Cicero. It's seasoned with fennel, pepper, *peperoni cruschi* (crushed peppers), and eaten fresh after roasting on a coal fire, but is also dried or preserved in olive oil.

Though it's now popular all over Italy, *soppressata* is also said to originate in Basilicata; it's made here with pasture-grazed pork from Rivello, which is dried and pressed, or kept in extra-virgin olive oil. *Pezzenta* (meaning, literally, 'beggars') is another salumi made from pork scraps and the smoky local Senise peppers.

Given the sparing use of meat in the diet here, cheese provides another valuable source of protein and is typically made from sheep and goat's milk. Cacioricotta is a local soft sheep's cheese similar to ricotta, while Pecorino di Filiano is a DOP-protected hard cheese. Basilicata's most famous cheese, however, is Caciocavallo. The prized Podolica cows which provide the milk for Caciocavallo graze in herb-filled pastures, and the cheese has a correspondingly intense flavour.

ANCIENT AGLIANICO

Basilicata's wines of choice are reds made from the Aglianico grape, the best of which are grown in the Vulture region. The Aglianico grape is thought to have been introduced by the Greeks in the 7th or 6th century BCE; since then, vineyards have been planted all over the volcanic slopes of Monte Vulture between Melfi, Rapolla and Barile, where the wines were originally aged in caves. Aglianico grapes are one of the last non-dessert varieties to be harvested, with picking taking place in late October or early November; the wine they produce has intense chocolate, cherry and liquorice notes. They pair well with the roasted marroncino di Melfi, the prized local chestnuts from Melfi.

Don't Miss

➔ **Calzone di Verdura** Baked pizza dough folded over a filling of chard, peppers and raisins.

➔ **Ciammotta** Vegetable stew of fried aubergines, potatoes, tomatoes and peppers, seasoned with *peperoni cruschi*.

➔ **Ciaudedda Lucania** Braised artichokes stuffed with potatoes, onions, broad beans and salted pork.

➔ **Pasta mollicata** The region's signature pasta dish, served with a sauce of onion, tomato, stale bread and a splash of red wine.

➔ **Spezzatino di agnello** Tougher cuts of lamb, stewed in a traditional earthenware pot with potatoes, onions, bay leaves and peppers.

➔ **Rafanata** An unusual frittata made with egg, potato, pecorino and grated horseradish – the latter is often referred to as the 'poor man's truffle'.

Left: A coastal view of Tropea in Calabria

CALABRIA

With fish from its long coastline, meat from its mountainous interior and an abundance of vegetables, Calabrian cuisine incorporates some unique ingredients: super spicy *peperoncini* (chillies), sweet Tropea onions, herbaceous liquorice and aromatic bergamot.

SIGNATURE FLAVOURS

Like nearby Puglia and Basilicata, Calabrian cooking originates in the tradition of *cucina povera* (poor man's food): vegetables and pasta feature in abundance, while fish and meat are highly prized and treated with much respect. That said, there are a number of typical ingredients here that might strike travellers as rather exotic. Chief among them is the chilli, introduced from the New World in the 16th century and now an integral part of Calabrian cooking. Add to that the region's famously sweet Tropea onions, and 'nduja, a soft, wet pork sausage packed with hot chilli. Calabrian kitchens cook up plenty of seafood (as in Sicily, swordfish is the most highly

prized fish), and the region is also known for its cured meats (mainly pork, veal and goat), but vegetables are also central to the cuisine here. Tomatoes, peppers and aubergines grow well in the mild climate, and appear in signature sauces such as *alla ghiotta* (tomato-based

and flavoured with capers, anchovies, garlic, olives, pine nuts and raisins), which forms a popular accompaniment to swordfish steaks. Vegetables are also preserved *sott'oli*, literally 'under oil', so they can be eaten throughout the year.

However, the standout Calabrian vegetable is the *cipolla Rossa di Tropea*, a deliciously sweet purple allium. Contrary to what you might think, the sweetness isn't due to a high sugar content; instead, a low volume of pyruvic acid dispenses with the harsh, pungent flavour of normal

'NDUJA

'Nduja is loosely modelled on the French andouille *sausage. Although 'nduja is eaten all over the region, it's thought to have originated in Spilinga, a village surrounded by chestnut forests where the local Nero di Calabria pigs forage freely. They provide the essential sausage meat (traditionally the offal and cheapest cuts), which is then spiced with chilli and encased in the pig's stomach before being smoked, cured and dried. The resulting salumi is a moist, spreadable pâté; versions vary in levels of spice.*

onions and lets the natural sugars shine through. Tropea onions come in three distinct varieties: the purple-red *cipolla fresca*, which are harvested in April; *cipolla da serbo*, harvested in June and with a more distinctively crimson tinge; and the white *cipollotto*, picked in October and resembling a large spring onion. Tropea onions are used in absolutely everything here, from sandwiches, pasta and salad dishes to marmalades and frittatas, as well as being served raw, grilled, roasted and salt-baked.

PASTA AND PITTA

Along with vegetables, Calabrian cooking features filling pastas such as *lagane e cicciari* (wide ribbons of pasta cooked with chickpeas and rosemary), and *ravioli Calabrese* (ravioli stuffed with the local Provola cheese, pecorino and *soppressata* salumi, and dressed in spicy tomato sauce). Meat ragù sauces tend to appear on festival days or for celebrations, and include highlights such as pasta *o' fùrnu*: rigatoni dressed with ragù and then layered with sliced aubergines, meatballs, cheese, cured meats and hard-boiled eggs.

Otherwise, Calabrians have a penchant for pitta, a bread-dough

stuffed with different fillings in the manner of a pie or calzone. There are savoury versions stuffed with meat, cheese and vegetables, and sweet versions, such as pitta *'mpigliata* (originally made for large celebrations and weddings), which is filled with dried fruits, spices and liqueurs. The inclusion of nuts and sweet dried fruits in *'mpigliata* demonstrates the Arab influence in many of Calabria's desserts.

CALABRIA'S FRAGRANT CITRUS

Anyone who's enjoyed the fragrant aroma of top quality Earl Grey tea will know the sweet scent of *bergamotto di Calabria*. Some 90% of the world's bergamot crop grows here, its oil extracted for food products and for perfumes and liqueurs. A little bigger than an orange, with a thin, knobbled green or yellow skin, it has an aromatic scent and flesh that is far too sour to eat

raw. The origins of the bergamot are hazy – some say it arrived in Italy from China, others elsewhere in Asia, or even Greece or Spain – and it's unclear as to whether it's a distinct species rather than an orange-lemon hybrid. Nonetheless, the plant thrives in Calabria's clay soils and through its long, hot summers – Reggio Calabria, the region's largest city, is known as the 'city of bergamot'.

Although bergamot has been used in herbal remedies for centuries – it's said to help with skin ailments, insomnia and colds – it wasn't until perfumer Johann Maria Farina employed it in his popular Eau de Cologne in 1709 that the fruit came to the world's attention. Today, as well as being an essential element of Earl Grey and other teas, it also features in numerous Calabrese pastries, cakes and desserts, as well as the Il Bergamino liqueur, homemade in kitchens throughout the region. In addition, you can find bergamot marmalade, jams, sweets, honey, vodka, gelato and the delicious bergamot granita.

CALABRIAN LIQUORICE

Calabria's mineral-rich clay soils offer ideal conditions for the liquorice plant (glycyrrhiza glabra), and the roots grown here are considered to be some of the best in the world. The plant is native to southern Europe and Southeast Asia – in China and Greece, its roots have been used to treat liver disease, food poisoning and coughs for centuries. Where other liquorice producers around the world supplement the roots with sugar to enhance the production of glycyrrhizic acid, which gives it the characteristic bittersweet, salty flavour, Calabrian liquorice is entirely natural. Amarelli is the oldest producer in the region – look out for their range of beautifully packaged spezzatine (boiled sweets), as well as liquorice-flavoured chocolate, liqueurs and even pasta.

Above: Typical Nduja sausage

Don't Miss

◆ **Licurdia** A simple soup of Tropea onions, grated potatoes and a pinch of chilli flakes.

◆ **Ravioli alla Calabrese** Ravioli filled with pecorino and provola cheeses, eggs and *soppressata* salumi, dressed in a spicy tomato sauce.

◆ **Pitta china Calabrese** A pizza-pie filled with salami, mozzarella, salted ricotta, Tropea onions, eggs and basil.

◆ **Pesce spada alla ghiotta** Sautéed swordfish steaks in a tomato sauce flavoured with Tropea onion, garlic, anchovies, pine nuts, capers and raisins.

◆ **Polpette alla Mammolese** Pork and goat meatballs in a spicy tomato sauce.

◆ **Tartufo di Pizzo** Two flavours of ice-cream around a centre of runny chocolate or fruit syrup, all encased in a chocolate shell.

SiCiLY

Sicilian cuisine stands out for its exoticism and uniqueness. Fish and shellfish form the foundation of food on the island, alongside a profusion of top quality fruit and vegetables, but you'll also see saffron, pistachio, rosewater and cinnamon – perhaps not the most obvious things you'd associate with Italian food.

A HISTORIC MELTING POT

Thanks to its strategic location at the centre of the Mediterranean, Sicily has been colonised by a whole panoply of peoples over the centuries, from the ancient Sicani and Phoenicians to the Greeks, Romans, Arabs, French and Spanish. The result is one of the most unique cultures and cuisines in Europe, blending eastern and western culinary techniques and flavours along with Islamic, Jewish and Christian traditions to form a distinct, sweet-and-sour palate based on an impressive larder of fresh ingredients.

Sicilian cuisine only really took shape after the arrival of Arab colonisers, collectively known as Saracens. As experienced agronomists and botanists, they saw great potential in the island's fertile land and brought with them new crops – such as citrus fruit and today's ever-present aubergine (eggplant) – as well as sophisticated methods of irrigation and farming. They introduced pasta to the island, as well as different ways of preparing food, combining nuts, dried fruits, meats, vegetables, herbs and spices. Thanks to their legacy, many classic Sicilian dishes combine currants and pine nuts, lemon peel, cinnamon and sugar, and nowhere else in Italy is mint used so extensively in cooking.

Another Arab influence is the couscous that you'll see on many menus in western Sicily; the Saracens also greatly extended the Romans' cultivation of rice, which today's Sicilians use to stuff vegetables or mould around fillings for *arancini* (deep-fried balls of rice flavoured with saffron, tomatoes, vegetables and meat) and *tummàla* (timbale), a sumptuous baked rice dish with chicken, eggs and cheeses, usually prepared around Christmas. On top of all this, the Saracens brought sugar cane to these shores, helping Sicilians to develop some of the best sweets in Italy.

SEAFOOD STAPLES

Unsurprisingly for a Mediterranean island, fish is at the heart of Sicilian cuisine. Although there is an abundance of seafood, the most highly prized species are tuna, sardines, anchovies and swordfish (the latter being, sadly, overfished these days). Because fish is so fresh

here, it is often eaten raw (*crudo*); if not, it's usually prepared simply or stuffed with anything from pine nuts and raisins to ricotta.

An iconic island favourite is *sarde a beccafico alla Palermitana* (sardines stuffed with anchovies, pine nuts, currants and parsley), but the filet mignon of the Sicilian marine world is *pesce spada* (swordfish), served either grilled with lemon, olive oil and oregano, or as *involtini* (slices of swordfish with cheese rolled around a spicy filling of onions, currants, pine nuts and breadcrumbs). Sardines feature in the iconic pasta *con le sarde*, in which sardines, wild mountain fennel (unique to Sicily), onions, pine nuts and raisins combine to create a wonderfully exotic flavour. The best swordfish is caught in Messina, where they serve the classic *agghiotta di pesce spada* (also called *pesce spada alla Messinese*), a mouthwatering dish flavoured with pine nuts, sultanas, garlic, basil and tomatoes.

GELATO & GRANITA

The peak of Mt Etna is a natural freezer; the Romans and Greeks used it to chill their wine. But it was the Arabs who started the Sicilian mania for all things icy with shahbah, flavoured fruit syrups mixed with iced water. Over time this evolved to sorbet, then granita (crushed ice mixed with fruit juice, coffee or almond milk) and cremolata (fruit syrups with iced milk), and from there to gelato (ice-cream). Ice-cream is not an apt translation, since Sicilian gelato is made not with cream but with biancomangiare (blancmange), an island staple for centuries.

The offshore Egadi Islands are known for two splendid tuna dishes: *tonno 'nfurnatu* (oven-baked tuna with tomatoes, capers and green olives) and *alalunga di Favignana al ragù* (fried albacore served in a spicy sauce of tomatoes, red chilli peppers and garlic); the latter sauce also appears regularly as part of pasta dishes. Look out, too, for calamari or *totani* (squid) and *calamaretti* (baby squid), which are served stuffed, fried, roasted or cooked in a tomato sauce. You'll also find plenty of *cozze* (mussels) and *vongole* (clams), as well as gamberi (shrimp), of which the most famous variety is *gamberi rossi di Mazara* (red shrimp from Mazara del Vallo).

SWEET TOOTH

Sicily is famous for its sweets and pastries. *Cassata* is the queen of Sicilian desserts, a rich cake made with ricotta, sugar, vanilla, diced chocolate and candied fruits. The equally famous *cannoli*, pastry tubes filled with sweetened ricotta, are found pretty much everywhere. Another ubiquitous treat is *frutta martorana*. Shaped to resemble fruits (or whatever takes the creator's fancy), these marzipan confections are part of a local tradition that dates back to the Middle Ages. In late October, they're sold in stalls around Palermo in anticipation of Ognissanti (All Souls' Day).

Also worth sampling are *paste di mandorla* (almond cookies), *gelo di melone* (watermelon jelly), *biscotti regina* (sesame-coated biscuits), *cassatelle* (pouches of dough stuffed with sweetened ricotta and chocolate), *cuccia* (made with wheatberries, honey and ricotta), and *sfogli polizzani* (a pastry of chocolate, cinnamon and fresh sheep's milk cheese). While in the Madonie region, make sure to try sweets made from *manna*, the edible sap harvested from ash trees around Castelbuono; and in Modica, seek out the local chocolate. Laced with spicy peppers it's based on an Aztec recipe brought here from Mexico when Sicily was under Spanish rule.

Don't Miss

➔ **Caponata** A sweet-and-sour salad made with aubergines, tomatoes, celery, capers, olives and onions seasoned with vinegar.

➔ **Arancini** Deep-fried balls of rice filled with ricotta, vegetables or a beef ragù and dusted with breadcrumbs.

➔ **Involtini di pesce spade** Rolls of swordfish stuffed with breadcrumbs and cheese.

➔ **Pasta alla Norma** A signature Sicilian dish: pasta (often rigatoni) in a sauce of tomato, basil and fried aubergine, topped with salted ricotta.

➔ **Falsomagro** A stuffed roll of minced beef, sausages, bacon, egg and pecorino cheese.

➔ **Cannoli** A deep-fried pastry tube piped full of creamy ricotta and finished with cocoa, crushed pistachio or citrus peel.

DESSERT WINES

Sicilian dessert wines are well worth buying to take home. Top of the list are sweet Marsala wines: the best labels are Florio and Pellegrino. Sweet Malvasia, from the Aeolian island of Salina, is a honey-sweet wine whose notable producers include Hauner, Virgona and Fenech. Italy's most famous Moscato (Muscat), made from Zibibbo grapes, is the Passito di Pantelleria from the island of the same name; it has a deep-amber colour and an extraordinary taste of apricots and vanilla. Donnafugata is Pantelleria's most prominent producer.

Left: A fishmonger with swordfish at Catania fish market

Left: A belltower
looking over Cagliari

SARDiNiA

Lobster, red prawns and mullet from the Med, wild thyme, rosemary, myrtle and juniper, sun-ripened olives, sweet and nutty pecorino, farm-raised lamb and suckling pig cooked on an open spit – nowhere does slow food like Sardinia.

SHEPHERDS, NOT FISHERMEN

Sardinians point out that they are, by tradition, 'pastori, non pescatori' ('shepherds, not fishermen'). There are more than 4 million sheep in Sardinia, so you'll see plenty of lamb and mutton, as well as pork and goat-meat. Younger animals are often eaten in simple ways – grilled over an open fire, perhaps – whilst older specimens end up as delicious stews or charcuterie such as prosciutto, pancetta and coppa. The mountainous eastern province of Barbagia is known for pecora in cappotto, a hearty mutton stew, while Nuoro province is famous for culurgiones de l'Ogliastra, pasta stuffed with potato puree and sometimes meat and onions. The region also produces the island's best-known red wines from the

Cannonau vine, which are especially good paired with roasted meats.

As to meats roasted on the spit and flavoured with Mediterranean herbs, three island specialities stand out: porceddu (suckling pig), agnello (lamb) and capretto (kid). The most famous of this culinary triumvirate is the porceddu which, as maialino arrosto, is slow-roasted until the skin crackles and the meat is meltingly tender, then left to stand on a bed of myrtle leaves. Lamb is popular around December and Easter, while kid is more common up in the mountains, where it is usually flavoured with thyme. A country classic – and a rarity – is su carraxiu (literally 'of the buried'), where the meat is compressed between two layers of hot stones, covered in myrtle and left to cook slowly in a hole dug in the ground. Game birds, rabbit and

wild boar also feature in season, often served with a tangy al mirto (red myrtle) sauce.

ANCIENT CHEESES

Given this is an island of shepherds, it's hardly surprising that Sardinians have a special affinity for cheese, which has been produced here for some 5000 years. Sardinia makes about 80% of Italy's pecorino (sheep's milk cheese), and gourmands will delight in its many flavours and textures, from tangy Pecorino Sardo to smoked varieties.

NOWHERE does SLOW FOOD like SARDINIA

MUSIC PAPER

As crisp as a cracker, pane carasau – *also known as* carta da musica *(music paper) – is the star of Sardinia's bread basket. Found particularly in the Gallura, Logudoro and Nuoro regions, it's still made by hand using durum wheat, water and a pinch of salt, and twice baked in a wood-fired oven. Brushed with olive oil and sprinkled with salt,* pane carasau *becomes a moreish snack known as* pane guttiau. *A fancier version is called* pane frattau, *where it's topped with tomato sauce, grated pecorino and a soft-boiled egg.*

There are also ricottas, creamy goat's cheeses such as Ircano and Caprino, and speciality cheeses like the sweet, tangy sheep- and goat-milk Canestrato.

Made to a centuries-old recipe, Fiore Sardo is eaten fresh, smoked or roasted and packs a fair punch. It's traditionally made from sheep's milk, but varieties such as *fresa* and *peretta* are made from cow's milk. The most popular goat's cheese is Caprino, and the soft Crema del Gerrei is a combination of goat's milk and ricotta. Only the bravest connoisseurs will want to sample Formaggio Marcio or Casu Marzu, quite literally a 'rotten cheese' that contains live maggots! Unsurprisingly, it's not one you'll see on the supermarket shelves.

FISH

Historically, there is some tradition of seafood in Cagliari, Alghero, Cabras and other coastal towns, but elsewhere the habit arrived later or has evolved from foreign influences. Alghero is a top spot for sampling some of the island's finest seafood. Try *aragosta alla Catalana* (lobster with tomato and onion) and, during the March to April season, *ricci* (sea urchins). *Cassola* is a tasty fish soup; Castelsardo speciality *zuppa alla Castellanese* is similar, but with a distinct tomato edge.

Cagliari's long tradition of seafood cooking includes one of the most famous dishes based on the local *gattuccio di mare* (catfish). Clams, cockles, octopus and crab also feature, as do eels around the marshes of Cabras, the latter sometimes served in Spanish-style *panadas* (mini pies similar to empanadas). For something more adventurous, try Olbia's *orziadas* (deep-fried sea anemones). Bluefin tuna (*tonno*) abounds around the Isola di San Pietro, while *muggine* (mullet) is the signature dish of Oristano. The *bottarga* (roe) obtained from grey mullet is emblematic of Sardinia's unique food traditions; it's usually served in thin slices as a starter or grated over pasta to add umami goodness.

Don't Miss

➔ **Burrida** Cagliari's signature dish: catfish marinated in garlic, vinegar, walnuts and spices.

➔ **Zuppa gallurese** A comfort food casserole comprising layers of bread, cheese and meat ragù, drenched in broth and baked to a crispy crust.

➔ **Maialino arrosto** Suckling pig wrapped in myrtle leaves and slow-cooked over juniper wood until meltingly tender.

➔ **Culurgiones** Hailing from Ogliastra, Sardinia's most famous pasta is usually stuffed with potato, pecorino and mint.

➔ **Fregola** A hand-rolled semolina pasta that looks like giant couscous. Often used in soups and salads, or flavoured with saffron and served with seafood.

➔ **Seadas** Deliciously light pastry turnovers stuffed with bran, orange peel and ricotta, or fresh pecorino drenched in *miele amaro* (bitter honey).

MIRTO

Mirto is Sardinia's national drink, a powerful liqueur distilled from the purple fruit of the myrtle bush. But Mirto is just the tip of the iceberg for Sardinian spirits. Islanders have developed a range of firewaters made using locally foraged ingredients, such as corbezzolo (an autumnal plant similar to a wild strawberry), prickly pears and basil. There's even a local form of limoncello, akin to the famous lemon-based tipple from the Amalfi Coast. The strangely named filu e ferru ('the iron wire') is similar to grappa. It is made from a distillate of grape skins and roars down the throat – the alcohol content hovers around 40%, with some home brews reaching 60%.

From left: A street cafe in Sardinia; Fregola with clams and mussels

Published in May 2021 by Lonely Planet
Global Limited CRN 554153
www.lonelyplanet.com
ISBN 978 18386 9049 6
© Lonely Planet 2020
10 9 8 7 6 5 4 3 2 1
Printed in Malaysia

Written by: Paula Hardy
Managing Director, Publishing: Piers Pickard
Associate Publisher: Robin Barton
Editors: Jessica Cole, Christina Webb, Nora Rawn, Polly Thomas
Art Direction: Daniel Di Paolo
Layout Designer: Tina García
Cover illustration: © Muti, Folio Art
Spot illustrations: Louise Sheeren, Tina García
Cartographer: Wayne Murphy
Print Production: Nigel Longuet

Lonely Planet offices
USA
230 Franklin Road, Building 2B, Franklin, TN 37064
T: 615-988-9713

IRELAND
Digital Depot, Roe Lane (off Thomas St),
Digital Hub, Dublin 8, D08 TCV4

STAY IN TOUCH lonelyplanet.com/contact